ELITE • 197

Russian Security and Paramilitary Forces since 1991

MARK GALEOTTI

ILLUSTRATED BY JOHNNY SHUMATE

Series editor Martin Windrow

OSPREY PUBLISHING
Bloomsbury Publishing Plc

Kemp House, Chawley Park, Cumnor Hill, Oxford OX2 9PH, UK
29 Earlsfort Terrace, Dublin 2, Ireland
1385 Broadway, 5th Floor, New York, NY 10018, USA
Email: info@ospreypublishing.com
www.ospreypublishing.com

OSPREY is a trademark of Osprey Publishing Ltd

First published in Great Britain in 2013

A CIP catalog record for this book is available from the British Library.

Print ISBN: 978 1 78096 105 7
ePDF: 978 1 78096 106 4
ePub: 978 1 78096 107 1

Editor: Martin Windrow
Index by Zoe Ross
Typeset in Sabon and Myriad Pro
Originated by PDQ Media, Bungay, UK
Printed and bound in Great Britain by
CPI (Group) UK Ltd, Croydon CR0 4YY

22 23 24 25 26   10 9 8 7 6 5

MIX
Paper | Supporting responsible forestry
FSC® C013604

Author's note

Translating out of Cyrillic always poses challenges. Apart from those in the Glossary below, I have chosen to transliterate names as they are pronounced (so, for example, the town of Orel is rendered as Oryol, and Ekaterinburg as Yekaterinburg). I have also ignored the diacritical "soft" and "hard" signs found in the original. The only exceptions are names that have acquired common forms in English – for example, I use the spelling "Gorbachev" rather than the phonetically correct "Gorbachov."

The Woodland Trust

Osprey Publishing supports the Woodland Trust, the UK's leading woodland conservation charity.

www.ospreypublishing.com

To find out more about our authors and books visit our website. Here you will find extracts, author interviews, details of forthcoming events and the option to sign-up for our newsletter.

Glossary of acronyms used in this text:

BON	*Brigada osobennogo naznacheniya* – Special Purpose Brigade (of Interior Troops)
FPS	*Federalnaya pogranichnaya sluzhba* – Federal Border Service
FSB	*Federalnaya sluzhba bezopasnosti* – Federal Security Service (formerly FSK)
FSIN	*Federalnaya sluzhba ispolneniya nakazanii* – Federal Penitentiary Service (lit., Federal Service for the Execution of Punishment)
FSK	*Federalnaya sluzhba kontrrazvedki* – Federal Counterintelligence Service (became FSB)
FSKN	*Federalnaya sluzhba po kontrolyu za oborotom narkotikov* – Federal Narcotics Control Service
FSO	*Federalnaya sluzhba okhrany* – Federal Protection Service
GNR	*Gruppa nemedlennogo reagirovaniya* – Rapid Response Group (of police)
GUVD	*Glavnoe upravlenie vnutrennykh del* – Main Internal Affairs Directorate (a major city police command)
KSN	*Komanda spetsialnogo naznacheniya* – Special Purpose Team (of police)
MUR	*Moskovskii ugolovnyi rozysk* – Moscow Criminal Intelligence (of Moscow GUVD)
MVD	*Ministerstvo vnutrennykh del* – Ministry of Internal Affairs
NP	*Nalogovaya politsiya* – Tax Police
OBrON	*Otdelnaya brigada osobennogo naznacheniya* – Independent Special Purpose Brigade (of Interior Troops)
ODON	*Otdelnaya diviziya osobennogo naznacheniya* – Independent Special Purpose Division (of Interior Troops)
OMON	*Otryad mobilnyi osobennogo naznacheniya* – Special Purpose Mobile Unit (of police)
OMSN	*Otryad mobilnyi spetsialnogo naznacheniya* – Special Purpose Unit (of police)
Opnaz	*Operativnogo naznacheniya* – Operational Purpose (Interior Troops)
OSN	*Otryad spetsialnogo naznacheniya* – Special Purpose Detachment (of Interior Troops)
PO	*Pogranichnyi okrug* – border district (also *pogranokrug*)
PPS	*Patrulno-postovaya sluzhba* – Patrol-Guard Service (of police)
PV	*Pogranichnye voiska* – Border Troops
RSN	*Rota spetsialnogo naznacheniya* – Special Purpose Company (of Interior Troops)
SBP	*Sluzhba bezopasnosti prezidenta* – Presidential Security Service
SKRF	*Sledstvennyi komitet RF* – Investigative Committee, Russian Federation
SMBP	*Spetsialnyi motorizovannyi batalon politsii* – Special Motorized Police Battalion (of Interior Troops)
SOBR	*Spetsialnyi otryad bystrogo reagirovaniya* – Special Rapid Response Detachment (of police)
Spetsgruppa	General term for a special forces group (plural, *spetsgruppy*)
Spetsnaz	*Spetsialnogo naznacheniya* – Special Purpose, i.e. special forces
TsSN	*Tsentr spetsialnogo naznacheniya* – Special Purpose Center
UVD	*Upravlenie vnutrennykh del* – Internal Affairs Directorate (local police command)
UVO	*Upravlenie vnevedomstvennoi okhrany* – Extradepartmental Guard Directorate (of police – "Okhrana")
UVO	*Upravlenie vnutrennei okhrany* – Internal Protection Directorate (of MVD – sometimes also *Vokhr*)
VOkhr	*Vnutrennyaya okhrana* – Internal Security
VP	*Voennaya politsiya* – Military Police
VV	*Vnutrennye voiska* –- Interior Troops

CONTENTS

RUSSIAN SECURITY AND PARAMILITARY FORCES SINCE 1991

INTRODUCTION

Police junior NCO processing prisoners inside a bus after a mass arrest in Chechnya in 1999; his black beret and the right chest tab identify OMON. These riot units affected the black leather jacket for most of the 1990s and into the 2000s, but it is now rarely seen in large cities and is, indeed, something of the mark of a provincial cop. The English-language shoulder title, probably "TEAM SPECIAL," is an affectation typical of the 1990s. (Northfoto/Shutterstock.com)

Russia has a tradition of violent politics, in which internal security forces are often crucial: as the suppressors of revolution, the eyes and strong right hands of the state, and the agents of factional politics – both as king-makers, and king-breakers. This is an age-old tradition, dating back to the custom of every medieval Rus' prince to maintain his *druzhina* or armed personal retinue, as well as to the *streltsy* ("shooters") raised by Ivan the Terrible in the 16th century. These latter were simultaneously a war-fighting force, the palace guard, the Moscow police, and even the fire brigade.[1] Later, the tsars would not only form the uniformed Special Corps of Gendarmes to suppress dissent, but would also rely on regiments of Cossacks to put down riots and rebellions. The Bolshevik Revolution of 1917 did not end the tendency of Russia's rulers to raise and retain numerous, competing internal security forces; if anything, leaders became all the more concerned about the need to maintain a balance of power between rival praetorians in order to exclude the danger of coups. The Bolshevik leader Lenin was initially guarded by a special unit of Latvian riflemen, but in due course the Red Army, political police, and regular police would form a stable (if mutually suspicious) security structure in the capital.

Russia's paramilitary and security forces have always tended to be closer to the political leadership than the regular military. Indeed, their job was often to keep the soldiers in line – a technique perfected by Stalin, who unleashed the NKVD secret police on the Red Army in the purges of 1937. Their role has tended to be explicitly political, making them the instruments of the government (or powerful figures within it) rather than simple servants of any legal or constitutional order. Having been its most vicious defenders, however, it was, ironically, their actions – and inactions – that proved pivotal in the downfall of the Soviet Union. In August 1991, Communist Party hardliners launched a political coup against President Gorbachev during his absence from Moscow. However, the refusal of members of the KGB's Alpha counterterrorist commando force to obey their orders and spearhead an

The closing years of the USSR saw the Kremlin trying to adapt to a new age of public protests for which it had never seriously planned. These police, present at an antigovernment march in 1991, are equipped with firefighters' helmets, clumsy body armor over their greatcoats, plastic shields that tended to buckle under impact, and rubber truncheons. Their main handicap, however, was that they had little real idea of what to do when public protests turned violent. (Author's photo)

attack on the parliamentary building used as a headquarters by maverick Russian leader Boris Yeltsin spelled the beginning of the end of the coup. In September 1993, however, after the dissolution of the USSR, security troops of the Ministry of Internal Affairs (MVD) would assault that same White House, this time on Yeltsin's orders, to forcibly close down the parliament that was defying him.

With the partition of the Soviet Union and the creation of an independent Russian Federation, President Yeltsin promised democratization and demilitarization, but his years in office (1991–99) proved to be a time of drift and disorder during which the security apparatus became increasingly important. In 1991, not counting the regular police, there had been more than 400,000 internal security troops and paramilitaries across the whole USSR – one for every 700 Soviet citizens, and one for every ten regular soldiers. By 1995 there were some 382,500 security and paramilitary troops in the Russian Federation alone, or one for every 392 citizens. The regular military was in a catastrophic state; while on paper it still had a strength of 1.9 million, there were fewer than a million actually at operational readiness. In other words, there was one security or paramilitary officer for every two or three truly deployable soldiers.

These security and paramilitary personnel may have been numerous, but they were not necessarily especially proficient. They were responsible for both blunders and brutality in the First Chechen War (1994–96), and have a distinctly mixed record in facing subsequent terrorist attacks. In part this reflects the need to do more with less, for while their duties were expanding their funding was shrinking. As a result, they suffered a hemorrhage of many of their most able officers into the private sector.

1 See Men-at-Arms 367, *Medieval Russian Armies 1250–1500*, and MAA 427, *Armies of Ivan the Terrible*

The impact of Putin

However, the rise of KGB veteran Vladimir Putin, President of Russia 2000–2008 and again since 2012, saw a revival in their fortunes. These agencies assumed a key role in the Second Chechen War (1999–2009), were increasingly lionized in the state-controlled media, and received steadily increasing budgets. Although Dmitry Medvedev was nominally president in the years 2008–12, Putin remained in charge behind the scenes as his powerful prime minister, and the security agencies have thus enjoyed more than a decade of expansion and generous funding.

Although some of these resources did trickle down to the regular police and paramilitary troops of the MVD, the disproportionate beneficiaries were the security services – above all the Federal Security Service (FSB), the main heirs to the KGB – and the numerous elite forces known by the umbrella term *Spetsnaz*. This term has been popularized mainly in connection with the Army's commando units, but in fact it is simply a contraction of *spetsialnogo naznacheniya*, "of special purpose," and is of more general application. The proliferation of such units in part reflects the increasingly complex challenges facing the country, from terrorism to organized crime. However, their growth has also been a product of the nature of Russian politics, as many agencies, often with overlapping and competing agendas, sought to assert their rights and roles. (For example, the struggle against drug-traffickers was a core responsibility of no fewer than four agencies – the MVD, the FSB, the Border Guards, and the Federal Narcotics Control Service – each with their own special forces.)

By the time of Putin's return to the Kremlin in 2012 this pattern had been set, and none of the agencies looked willing to give up their *spetsgruppy* – their special forces groups. If anything, these continue to multiply, as new ones are established at local levels. Russia is, after all, the largest country in the world, comprising 83 separate constituent republics and regions, and spanning nine time zones. In such a country the ability to draw on local forces – familiar with conditions in their home regions, and, above all, based closer than several hours' flight-time away – is often crucial. More to the point, as a growing proportion of Afghan heroin moves north through Russia, as insurgency spreads in the North Caucasus, and as the threat of political disorder grows, the Kremlin is likely to see its need for these elite security and paramilitary forces increase rather than diminish.

The uniform of the regular police in early 2012, before the issue of the more modern and less military design (see Plate A1). The red cap band and piping stand out against the dark gray and black of this spring/fall uniform. The Ministry of Internal Affairs (MVD) crest on the crown of the cap features the traditional Russian double-headed eagle, and the badge on the band has the Russian tricolor cockade – blue, white, and red, from edge to center – set in a wreath. The silver-gray central motif on the right-sleeve patch identifies the exact arm of service. (Lilyana Vynogradova/Shutterstock.com)

BELOW
Mounted policewoman from the Moscow force, the blue-gray uniform modified to include riding breeches and high black boots; she carries a longer baton than regular foot officers, to give her a longer reach from the saddle. As in other countries, mounted police are essentially used in public-order and ceremonial roles, and also tend to be very smartly turned out. (Mikhail Olykainen/Shutterstock.com)

MVD FORCES:

THE POLICE

The Russian Ministry of Internal Affairs (*Ministerstvo vnutrennykh del*, MVD) is one of the so-called "power ministries" that have historically been key institutions of state control, and it has grown in strength and prestige during Putin's reign as president and prime minister. Though never as politically significant as the intelligence and internal security agencies, the MVD saw its funding rise steadily in line with growing federal budgets, fueled by taxes on oil and gas revenues. As well as underpinning a substantial force of internal security troops, these have funded the country's extensive police forces, including specialized paramilitary elements within them. Although formally each constituent republic of the Russian Federation has its own interior ministry, in practice they are usually little more than local satellites of the main MVD in Moscow. Beneath these are a network of local Internal Affairs Directorates (*Upravlenii vnutrennykh del*, UVD), with some Main Internal Affairs Directorates (*Glavnye upravlenii vnutrennykh del*, GUVD) for larger cities such as Moscow and St Petersburg.

A corpulent captain of the much-maligned DPS traffic police, his branch identified by his light gray cap band and the tab above the shield on his left breast. Compare this blue spring/fall uniform with the winter outfit, Plate A2; both feature reflective strips around the sleeves, and both men have the black-and-white baton. His shoulder boards of rank, with red piping and four gold stars, are very similar to the military design. The left-sleeve shield shows "ROSSIYA" and "MVD" above and below the national tricolor – see Plate A, inset 2a. (Denis Klimov/Shutterstock.com)

From *militsiya* to *politsiya*

The regular police were known until 2011 by their Soviet name of *militsiya*, "militia," reflecting their Revolutionary origins in *ad hoc* groups of armed Bolshevik workers and soldiers. During the Soviet era they quickly reverted to a traditional Russian pattern, becoming a formalized, bureaucratic, professional armed police service, responsible above all for enforcing the laws and discipline of the state rather than for protecting the rights of the individual. In everything from their uniforms to their rank structure they echoed the Red Army; indeed, the military was also involved in police work, from suppressing disturbances to providing manpower for major manhunts. A combination of political immunity, low pay, and a lack of independent checks and balances ensured that the militia not only lacked public legitimacy but also became infamously corrupt. It became common practice, for example, to leave a suitable-denomination banknote tucked inside your driving license for the next time a traffic officer waved you down on some spurious grounds. While there undoubtedly were able and efficient officers and investigators, they were constrained by a culture of obsessive paperwork and political sensitivity.

When the Soviet Union collapsed there was widespread optimism that major change would come to the militia. In practice, however, the new Yeltsin regime had neither the money nor the interest to reform the MVD. (It was only in 2004, for example, that the police officially shed their role, long since ignored in practice, of monitoring color-copying facilities – a relic of the Soviet regime's paranoia about their use to spread subversive literature.)

A

POLICE & POLICE AUXILIARIES
(1) Police patrol officer, 2012
This officer, in the new medium-weight spring and fall service uniform which began to be issued in 2012, is from the Patrol-Guard Service (PPS), the main street police force. Engaged in routine vehicle stop-and-search duties, he nevertheless carries a 9mm PP-2000 submachine gun. At his belt he would also carry a holstered Yarygin PYa pistol and a PR-73M rubber truncheon. He is unusually by-the-book in his appearance, even carrying his identity card visible on his right breast – as required by law, but still relatively rare. This would suggest that he is newly trained under the revised curriculum introduced in 2011. He displays the MVD cockade badge on his cap, a police patch on his right sleeve, and a "POLITSIYA" tab and his shield on his left chest.

(2) Traffic policeman; St Petersburg, 2011
This rather less impressive officer of St Petersburg's State Traffic Safety Inspectorate (*Gosudarstvennaya inspectsiya bezopasnosti dorozhnogo dvizheniya*, GIBDD) wears the winter uniform of a blue jacket with reflective bands and patches, and matching trousers; note the collar faced with synthetic

fleece, and the zip-together hood thrown back. On his right sleeve is the St Petersburg GIBDD patch, on his left the MVD patch with the Russian tricolor **(inset 2a)**, and on his left chest the traffic police tab and his shield. He carries a personal radio, and a black-and-white baton – used for directing traffic, but also with a secondary self-defense function. Given that he is on duty in a busy city center, he has not been issued the PB-4SP OSA "traumatic pistol" sometimes carried by traffic police.

(3) Cossack junior lieutenant; Magadan, 2012
In 2012 the Magadan UVD in the Russian Far East established a program to allow volunteers from the Ussuri Cossack Host to sign up as police auxiliaries. This junior lieutenant from Kolyma district wears a uniform reminiscent of the tsarist era, with modern police rank badges, the MVD patch on his left sleeve, and an Ussuri Cossack Host patch on the right. Officially he should not be armed, but he carries an Army-surplus Makarov PM in a non-standard cross-draw holster on an old-fashioned leather belt-and-yoke set; he would also have a homemade wooden baton at his other hip. Kolyma is the site of several hard-labor camps, and the tattoo on his wrist suggests that this law-enforcer once served time in one of them.

1

2a

РОССИЯ

МВД

2

3

A beat cop of the Patrol-Guard Service in Moscow, 2012. The patch on the back of the body-armor vest still reads "*Militsiya*" even though the force was formally renamed *Politsiya* more than a year before. He has a holstered PMM pistol on his right hip, and a baton on his left. (Author's photo)

RIGHT
A police dog-handler in winter uniform, the garments in various shades of blue-gray. The leather satchel on his right hip holds documents and notebook; the canvas haversack is for supplies for his remarkably relaxed-looking dog, which is a graduate of the MVD's Central Region Cynological Service. (Olga Lis/Shutterstock.com)

FAR RIGHT
Senior police officers confer near Red Square on the morning of President Putin's third inauguration in March 2012. The central officer, with red-edged epaulets on his black leather coat and a double red trouser-stripe, is a major-general. He is flanked by a lieutenant-colonel (left) and a colonel of the traffic police, with large reflective Cyrillic "DPS" initials on the backs of their jackets. The colonel and major-general have more luxurious fleece caps and collars than the lieutenant-colonel, in gray lambskin. (Author's photo)

The unreformed and neglected militia found itself struggling to cope with a new era of rising organized crime with shrinking budgets and no clear leadership from the Kremlin. To a considerable extent the police withdrew even further from society, engaging in a process of impromptu "paramilitarization"; it became commonplace to see traffic police toting submachine guns, and local stations sometimes resembled bunkers. This was also a time of increasing criminalization of the police, with officers engaging not just in petty bribe-taking but working for organized crime-lords or forming their own gangs. Even efforts to bring in revenue by hiring out police through the Extradepartmental Guard Service (*Vnevedomstvennaya okhrana*) proved problematic. When the alleged organized-crime boss Vasili Naumov was assassinated in 1997, for example, it emerged that his bodyguards were members of "Saturn," an elite St Petersburg police unit, who had been hired through a front company. It is hardly surprising that most surveys put the level of public trust in the police at around 10–20 percent only.

Under Putin, resources once again began to be allocated to the police, but there was no substantive reform. Instead, it was during the single term in which he retreated to the position of prime minister (as the Russian constitution forbade anyone serving three consecutive terms as president), with his client Dmitry Medvedev as titular president (2008–12), that this process began. A lawyer by training, Medvedev appreciated the problems with Russian law enforcement. He introduced a new Law on the Police in 2011, which not only changed the force's name back to *politsiya*, "police," but also mandated compulsory re-accreditation of all serving officers, with the aim of cutting the size of the force by 22 percent to 1,106,472 officers. At the same time, salaries were to be increased by 30 percent. It remains to be seen whether or not this will prove an essentially cosmetic exercise in rebranding, but there are some indications that the Russian police are beginning, slowly, to change.

Organization

The police are largely organized under local UVDs and GUVDs, each in turn divided into a wide range of constituent divisions, from criminal investigations through to traffic duties. A distinctive element of the Russian police model is the presence of "precinct inspectors," who live in the large housing estates which are such a feature of Russian cities, and whose apartments also double as police stations.

Moscow, unusually, has two elements, the 1st and 2nd Operational Regiments, which bridge the gap between regular police and the more muscular OMON riot police and the Interior Troops (both discussed below). Each over a thousand strong, the Operational Regiments have specialized public-order roles, and are subordinated to UOOP, the Moscow GUVD's Public-Order Directorate. The 1st Regiment also includes the city's mounted police, and provides additional patrollers on the streets; the 2nd is tasked primarily with handling major public events and disturbances. Overall, the capital's public-order forces are coordinated from the Special Reaction Force Operations Center, established at Strogino on Moscow's outer ring road in 2010 under Maj Gen Vyacheslav Khaustov. The Center's role is to prevent and disperse unauthorized public gatherings and to suppress disorder, and it is expected that similar operational command posts may be set up in other key cities. Beyond the UVDs and GUVDs, there are also a range of other specialized police departments for the transport network and other institutions.

Officers of Moscow's 1st Operational Regiment (see right chest tab), a special police unit that provides additional manpower and support for regular operations. The right-sleeve patch with an eagle central motif denotes their subordination to UOOP, the police's Directorate for the Protection of Public Order; the usual MVD patch is worn on the left sleeve. The two stars on his epaulet identify the foreground man as a *praporshchik* or warrant officer. (Author's photo)

LEFT
The MVD is increasingly recruiting women into the ranks, even of the more combative arms such as OMON and, as here in May 2010, Moscow's Operational Regiments. They wear gray mid-weight uniforms with red trouser piping. The black beret was originally limited to OMON riot police, but its use by this unit symbolizes a hybrid status, midway between regular and riot cops. (Hinochika/Shutterstock.com)

Police from Moscow's 2nd Operational Regt heading out to assist in a raid; note the helmets with camouflage covers. They are armed with truncheons and Makarov PM pistols as well as AKS-74U assault carbines. Not an ideal weapon for police, the latter are being replaced with 9mm PP-2000 and PP-19-01 submachine guns. (Vitaly Kuzmin)

BELOW
OMON riot police in 2011, wearing a mixture of old and new gear. Over their blue tiger-striped "urban" camouflage fatigues some wear body-armor vests in black, others in inappropriate green forest pattern. While their helmets are new, their metal riot shields date back to the 1980s. (Serge Lamere/Shutterstock.com)

Weapons

The police generally carry Makarov PM and PMM pistols, a compact but not especially accurate or effective weapon. The limitations of these standard sidearms help explain the militia's readiness in the 1990s to take up more lethal military-grade weapons (such as AKS-74U assault carbines), which were actually badly suited for regular police work: they intimidated the citizenry, lacked particular accuracy, and fired rounds that all too easily injured innocent bystanders by ricocheting or passing through their intended targets. As a result, in 2008 it was announced that the police would exchange their Makarovs and most Kalashnikov-based weapons (apart from those used by special units) for Yarygin PYa Grach pistols, and 9mm PP-2000 and PP-19-01 Vityaz submachine guns. The intention was that all officers would be re-equipped within three years, but, as tends to be the case in Russia, the reality lagged behind the plan. As of mid-2012 most officers, even in Moscow, still carried Makarovs, and AKS-74Us were still commonplace. However, over time new weapons are gradually being issued. Furthermore, precinct inspectors, traffic police and officers in similarly lower-hazard duties are being issued PB-4SP OSA pistols firing non-lethal rounds.

OMON

While the police are routinely involved in public-order duties, these and more serious armed-response operations are especially the preserve of the "black berets" of the OMON, the Special Purpose Mobile Units (*Otryady mobilnye osobennogo naznacheniya*). This name deserves brief explanation: the word *naznacheniye* means either "purpose" or "designation," and is frequently used in either sense in the nomenclature of Russian special and paramilitary units. The OMON were originally called the Special Purpose Militia Units (*Otryady militsii osobennogo nazanacheniya*), but with the renaming of the police in 2011 the question arose as to what to call them. Originally it was announced that each OMON would be rechristened a KON, Special Purpose Team (*Komanda osobennogo naznacheniya*), but this met with a distinct lack of enthusiasm. After lobbying from police and veterans' groups, in 2012 they received their current name, which retains their powerful – and intimidating – "brand name" acronym, and avoids the need for an expensive revision of their uniform insignia and vehicle liveries.

The *Omonovtsy* actively cultivate their reputation for ruthless efficiency, since it cements their *esprit de corps* and deters would-be protesters. They were created in Soviet times, reflecting a

OMON in Moscow's Bolotnaya Square during the opposition's "March of Millions" protest in May 2012. He wears a black mesh lightweight utility vest over Kora-Kulon body armor, as well as rigid shoulder, elbow, forearm, and leg protectors. The ski-mask balaclava worn under the riot helmet is a personal addition. (Nickolay Vinokurov/Shutterstock.com)

growing concern in the 1980s about a new threat of public disorder. They were the brainchild of Lev Zaikov, the Party boss of Leningrad (as St Petersburg was then called). When Zaikov was moved to Moscow in 1987 he brought his ideas with him, and the establishment of the Moscow OMON followed in November of that year, based on the city police's then-existing Operational Regiment. In 1988, the USSR MVD decreed that such units should be created throughout the Union, under the control of republican interior ministries.

In the closing years of Soviet power the OMON were to gain an unsavory reputation as the "stormtroopers of repression," being used against protesters around the USSR. Most notoriously, they were deployed to attack the Latvian Interior Ministry building in January 1991, killing six people, and border outposts of Lithuania, which had declared its independence. There were hopes that the new Yeltsin government would disband these units, but instead they continued to prosper. In 1993 Yeltsin even used them to help dissolve parliament during a constitutional crisis. At this point they were still primarily riot police; however, the onset of the First Chechen War in 1994 saw OMON from units throughout Russia being used increasingly as security forces or even frontline soldiers. In particular, they were used in the kind of operation known as a *zachistka*, a "clean-up," in which a village or neighborhood would be surrounded and then subjected to a house-by-house search. International observers have alleged that these operations frequently involve human-rights abuses and looting.

OMON were also used during the Second Chechen War (1999–2009). Perhaps because they were again drawn in contingents from numerous districts, with differing levels of training, they demonstrated a wide spectrum of capacities and qualities. Some were amongst the toughest and most professional federal forces in-theater, while others proved abusive or unprofessional. The majority of abuse cases reported to national and international human-rights monitors were blamed on OMON, although to a degree this simply reflects the extent to which they were used precisely for those operations involving direct contact with the civilian population.

There were also a number of "friendly-fire" incidents, the worst of which took place in the Chechen capital, Grozny, in March 2000. OMON from Podolsk ambushed a convoy of OMON from Sergiyev Posad coming to relieve them, believing them to be insurgents. In the ensuing firefight, which opened with a volley of rocket-propelled grenades and heavy machine-gun fire by

OMON practicing an assault on an upper-story window. Such operations are in fact rare, and in any case would be carried out using ladders, but Russian training programs for police and other special forces put great emphasis on developing physical strength, agility, and team spirit. This photo shows the Noch 91 blue camouflage fatigues to good effect, worn here with mismatched tactical/armor vests. (Northfoto/Shutterstock.com)

the ambushers, 22 of the 98 Sergiyev Posad *omonovtsy* were killed (including their commander, Col Dmitry Markelov) and more than 30 wounded; two of the Podolsk policemen were also killed. Despite an initial attempt by the authorities to cover this up as an insurgent attack, it was later admitted, and a public inquiry ultimately placed posthumous blame on Col Markelov.

OMON now have a variety of sometimes contradictory roles: as regular patrol officers, public-order and riot-control police, armed-response paramilitaries, and, in extreme cases, counterinsurgency special forces. There are OMON in every region of Russia and every major city: some 121 units were in existence as of 2007, with a total strength of over 20,000 *omonovtsy*. Unit sizes vary: Moscow's has over 2,000 officers, while in some cities they are no more than a company of 200–250 men. They share the same uniform

B

OMON & OMSN

(1) OMON Special Purpose Mobile Police officer, riot armor; Moscow, 2012
This "cosmonaut" of the Moscow City OMON (so nicknamed because the riot gear supposedly makes him look like a spaceman) is awaiting the order to disperse an antigovernment protest in Moscow's Pushkin Square. He is wearing black full-length KZS-Partner composite arm and leg protectors over the standard blue "urban" Noch camouflage fatigues, with a Kolpak 1-SB1 helmet. He is not carrying a firearm, which might be a danger or a temptation in a mêlée, but instead has a metal riot shield and a long, rigid, side-handled baton.

(2) OMSN operator; Penza, 2006
Each OMSN unit (since this date renamed KSN, Special Purpose Teams) tends to have its own distinct variations of uniform and equipment. This officer from Penza in southwestern Russia wears fatigues in the green "smog" camouflage reminiscent of the British DPM pattern, with a 6B23 armored vest and a

ZSh-1-2 steel helmet. His left-sleeve patch bears the tricolor and "UVD/Penza." The fingerless gloves are not standard issue, and the balaclava – a common item for troops engaged in operations against criminals and terrorists alike – is actually a motorcycle helmet liner. He is armed with an AKS-74U assault carbine and a holstered GSh-18 pistol.

(3) Female OMON K-9 officer; Astrakhan, 2011
This member of the small but growing minority of female OMON officers is a dog-handler in the southern Russian city of Astrakhan, where the local OMON unit has been dubbed Sapsan, "Peregrine Falcon." She is still armed with a Makarov PM pistol, although her German Shepherd dog is a rather more formidable asset. She wears the classic OMON black beret and blue "urban" camouflage fatigues, over a blue-and-white striped *telnyashka* T-shirt copied from military airborne and marine elites. She displays the MVD cap badge **(inset 3a)**, the Astrakhan OMON patch incorporating a black falcon on her right sleeve, the MVD patch on her left sleeve (see Plate A, inset 2a), and the "OMON" title on her right breast.

1

2

3a   3

An OMON Lavina-Uragan water cannon, built on the chassis of a Ural 532362 truck and here finished in Moscow police livery; note the city's St George and Dragon symbol on the red panel on the door. After using mostly fire engines in this role through the 1980s, Russia now produces some of the most powerful water cannon in the world. (Vitaly Kuzmin)

Chilly-looking young Moscow police officers wearing gray winter uniforms at a demonstration in December 2008. As is usual for such operations, they carry truncheons but not firearms. Their main role is to mark a perimeter; more seriously trained and equipped OMON are held in reserve to deal with any concerted efforts to break through such cordons. (Vitaly Kuzmin)

In major public-order incidents regular police may also be deployed directly against protesters; these officers are watching a gathering anti-Putin protest in Moscow's Pushkin Square. While equipped with helmets and basic body armor, they lack the advanced armor with arm and leg protectors issued to specialist units. The patch on the back of the vest reads "POLITSIYA." (Author's photo)

of blue-streaked Noch 91 "urban" camouflage fatigues and black beret, but details vary from unit to unit. Some have distinctive badges; others wear a blue-and-white striped *telnyashka* T-shirt under their jackets, a tradition that has crossed over from the regular military's paratroopers and marines. It used to be common for *omonovtsy* either to buy their own alternative uniforms or equipment or, in some cases, for local authorities or private sponsors to pay for these. Thus, many units deployed to Chechnya outfitted themselves in foreign-made camouflage uniforms and alternative helmets (the standard-issue ZSh-1-2 was widely considered too clumsy, and degraded hearing).

On the other hand, OMON tend to stick to their regular-issue weapons. Depending on their mission, they may carry riot truncheons and body armor or full paramilitary kit. Their regular weapons are 5.45mm AK-74 and AK-107 or 7.62mm AK-103 assault rifles (the last is sometimes favored because its older, larger round is deemed to have more stopping power), SVD sniper rifles, AKS-74U

assault carbines, numerous varieties of submachine gun including the 9A-91, PP-19 Bizon, and Kedr, and Makarov PMM or PYa Grach pistols. When on combat duty in the North Caucasus they add a full range of heavy support weapons, including GP-25 grenade-launchers, machine guns, and grenades. They also use BTR-series armored personnel carriers, although in their normal duties they rely on trucks, vans, and GAZ-233034 and GAZ-233036 SPM-2 Tigr ("Tiger") light armored vehicles. They also use a number of specialized vehicles, including the Abaim-Abanat assault vehicle fitted with an extending ramp for rapid boarding of hijacked aircraft or entry into the upper floors of a building, and water cannon, including the fearsome Russian-built Lavina-Uragan ("Avalanche-Hurricane").

Recruitment to the OMON and subsequent training places a considerable premium on physical strength and fitness. It is open to men between the ages of 22 and 30 who have successfully completed their national military service, and they may either apply directly or from within the police force. After a battery of tests including medical and psychological screening, they then undergo a four-month initial training course including marksmanship and unarmed combat, before being finally assessed for entry. However, training does not stop there, as *omonovtsy* spend more of their time in practice and drills than on police duties.

December 2010: Moscow City OMON, wearing Kora-Kulon armor vests, scuffling with protesters during a rally triggered by the death of a football fan in a brawl with rival youths from the North Caucasus. After a lull during the 1990s, recent years have seen an upsurge in intercommunal tensions. (kojoku/Shutterstock.com)

The Beslan massacre, September 2004

One of the most serious terrorist incidents in which the OMON were involved, alongside the pick of the other security special forces, took place in Beslan, a small town in North Ossetia close to the border with Chechnya. On September 1, 2004 about 34 hard-line Chechen insurgents from the Riyadus-Salikhin Battalion chose the first day of the school year to seize School Number One in the town. Of the 1,100 hostages taken, 777 were children. Under orders from Chechen warlord Shamil Basayev, who by this time had become associated with the Muslim fundamentalist wing of the rebels, they demanded a full withdrawal of Russian forces from Chechnya. Eighteen hostages were killed during the attack or shortly afterwards, and the terrorists then began turning the school into a fortress, installing boobytraps and constructing a snipers' nest on the roof. The hostages were herded into the school gymnasium, which was then rigged with explosives.

A massive security operation was launched. Initially, North Ossetian OMON established a perimeter; they were soon reinforced by other police and Interior Troops, as well as elite antiterrorist troops airlifted in, including the Federal Security Service's Alpha and Vympel units. Attempts were made to reach a compromise, including a face-to-face negotiation between the terrorists and Ruslan Aushev, a decorated veteran and former vice-president of Russia and president of Ingushetia. A few hostages were released, but it was clear that the terrorists were unwilling to accept anything short of a full Russian capitulation to their demands.

On the third day of the siege, as medical workers approached the school – with the terrorists' agreement – to remove the bodies of executed hostages, they came under fire. For reasons that are still unclear, two of the bombs in the gymnasium detonated, blowing out part of the wall. Some hostages were killed in the blast; others tried to flee and were fired on by the terrorists. The Russian commanders on the ground, FSB deputy directors Vladimir Pronichev and Vladimir Anisimov, decided that they could not wait any longer and signaled an assault, even though there was no clear

Russian OMON on active service in northern Chechnya during the First Chechen War (1994–96); the mismatch of camouflage fatigues with local conditions was reflective of the Russians' unpreparedness for this conflict. They are armed with AK-74 rifles and a PKM machine gun, and one carries what appears to be an RPG-7 HEAT round with a propellant charge tube taped to it. The left-hand man displays a yellow-on-black English-language shoulder title "TEAM SPECIAL"; such affectations were initially common (with or without grammatical errors), but nowadays are much less widely seen. (Northfoto/Shutterstock.com)

plan in place. What followed was a confused and bloody five-hour engagement, which saw terrorists using women and children as human shields, the Russians firing 125mm tank cannon and RPO-A incendiary rockets at the school to breach walls, and one insurgent almost being lynched by an angry mob when he tried to escape by pretending to be a fleeing hostage. While the Alpha and Vympel teams went into the school, the OMON were charged with overwatch (including neutralizing snipers) and maintaining a perimeter; for example, the terrorist who tried to flee was taken into custody by OMON officers, who came close to having to fire into the air to disperse the enraged locals.

These OMON riot police wear Maska-2 helmets, Noch camouflage fatigues with winter fleece collars, padded gloves, and rigid forearm protectors, and carry Vitrazh-AT shields. (Vitaly Kuzmin)

The butcher's bill was a grim one; about 12 policemen and soldiers died, including seven men from Vympel and three from Alpha. Of the 334 hostages killed, the largest proportion died when the gymnasium roof collapsed, but others were killed by terrorists or in the crossfire. The only terrorist known to have survived, the OMON's prisoner Nur-Pashi Kulayev, was later sentenced to life in a high-security facility. More generally, the Beslan siege proved a catalytic event for Russia's police and security apparatus. For the OMON, who felt that they had been relegated to an essentially passive role in the operation, it led to a series of initiatives. First of all, they began to acquire specialist hostage-negotiation experts: one clear finding of various inquiries after Beslan had been the relative inefficiency of efforts to gain time and concessions from the terrorists. Secondly, problems in coordinating operations between OMON from different commands encouraged a greater degree of standardization and cross-training. Finally, greater emphasis has since been placed on developing OMON snipers and specialist firearms units. Their main role remains the maintenance of public order, but after Beslan the OMON became more determined that in future terrorist crises they should be able to play a more productive and proficient role.

SOBRs, OMSNs, and KSNs

While the OMON are generally trained for both public-order and armed-response operations, there are also smaller specialist forces within the police. Although they are still often collectively described as *gruppy zakhvata*, "snatch squads," attesting to the more aggressive role they historically played, they are increasingly trained and employed not just for the detention of armed and dangerous suspects, but also in hostage-rescue, witness-protection, and similar roles. The titles of these (essentially similar) forces are Special Rapid Response Detachment (*Spetsialnyi otryad bystrogo reagirovaniya*, SOBR) and Special Purpose Police Detachment (*Otryad militsii spetsialnogo naznacheniya*, OMSN).

The first OMSN was established in 1980 within MUR, the Moscow police's criminal investigations division, and they later proliferated. Although many local police commands had a SWAT team, typically known as a Rapid Response Group (*Gruppa nemedlennogo reagirovaniya*, GNR), these were often of limited effectiveness, being simply ordinary beat officers who were given a little extra firearms training and pulled in from their regular duties when need arose. As the challenge of serious organized crime grew in the late 1980s and into the 1990s, more and more local forces came to recognize the need for true specialists, and began creating their own OMSNs. Most were formed during the early 1990s, and now every police command has at least one, usually with a distinctive name; for example, the Moscow unit is called Rys' ("Lynx"), the Mordovian team Zvezda ("Star"), and the Krasnoyarsk unit Zenit ("Zenith").

While OMSNs were typically assigned to commands responsible for criminal investigations or fighting organized crime, the more general term SOBR also emerged for similar units attached to different police departments. Generically, it is also sometimes used for special detachments in other agencies, such as the Justice Ministry and the former Tax Police. Precisely because of the confusion between the two terms, in 2002 erstwhile Interior Minister Boris Gryzlov ordered that all SOBRs be reclassified as OMSNs and subordinated to organized-crime departments. However, like many of his decrees, it was only partially obeyed at best, and SOBRs survive as of the time of writing, ten years later.

In 2011 it was announced that every OMSN would be renamed a Special Purpose Team (*Komanda spetsialnogo naznacheniya*, KSN) and, along with OMON, would be subordinated to regional Special Purpose Centers (*Tsentr spetsialnogo naznacheniya*, TsSN); whether this will actually be applied in practice remains to be seen. In Moscow, local units including the Zubr ("Bison") OMON, Rys' ("Lynx") KSN, and the MVD Interior Troops aviation assets have been combined into the MVD Center for Special Purpose Operational Reaction Forces and Aviation, directly subordinated to the ministry. However, if past experience is any guide, this kind of reform may well never reach the provinces.

Training and missions
Joining an OMSN, SOBR, or KSN team requires the applicant, whether already a police officer or not, to pass a tough series of physical and mental tests; typically, only 10–20 percent pass the selection process. They then receive extensive training that would be familiar to specialist officers in the West, although, as is usual in Russia, greater emphasis is placed on unarmed combat skills and physical strength. An operator's regular kit weighs 30kg (66lb), and he is expected to be able to run, rappel down buildings, or leap obstacles in this outfit. Moreover, he will often be wearing body armor and may well be carrying extra ammunition and equipment, so he may be carrying up to an 80kg (176lb) load. The exact nature of the load-out is mission specific; the level of equipment has also often varied depending on the wealth of the unit's home region, but by 2010 problems in the distribution of federal funds had largely been resolved, and even provincial units could afford modern kit. They increasingly favor black or camouflage assault fatigues, body armor, and the kinds of weapons used by OMON and counterterrorist units.

Given their specialist skill set, it is not surprising that OMSN and SOBR teams have seen service during the insurgencies in the North Caucasus. During both Chechen wars many were deployed as frontline combat troops, or in basic security roles such as manning vehicle checkpoints (something of a waste of their training), simply because of a shortage of effective combatants. This became a public scandal in 2002, when SOBR officers from the Volga city of Cherepovets issued an open letter complaining that they were not receiving combat pay for operations in Chechnya; were being used for inappropriate missions; and had just had the standard length of their posting to the war zone doubled, from 90 to 180 days. Special police from many other regions chimed in with similar complaints, while local authorities – resenting the Kremlin's blithe requisitioning of units that they had spent time and money training for their own law-enforcement needs – also began to complain, if more quietly.

The result was that these units began again to receive bonus pay and were treated with greater consideration. While many officers still had to serve extended tours in the war zone, at least they did find themselves generally used more selectively for specialist missions, something that has continued into the present era of insurgency. In 2011, for example, LtCol Mohammed Gayirkhanov was posthumously made a Hero of the Russian Federation – the country's highest military decoration – for bravery in an antiterrorist operation in the North Caucasus against local Islamist fighters. Formerly an officer in the Republic of Dagestan SOBR, he had then moved to the Republic of Kalmykia and rose to head its OMSN (known as Krechet, "Merlin") at the age of 36. In September 2010 Krechet was engaged in operations in Dagestan, and Gayirkhanov was handling negotiations with a group of fighters who had taken hostages in the village of Komsomolsk; when talks failed, he was fatally caught in the crossfire.

Russian special forces often train for rappelling down buildings, and insertions by helicopter, even though they rarely get the chance to do either in real operations. Here officers from the Moscow OMON's Zubr ("Bison") unit deploy from a police Aerospatiale AS-355N Ecureuil 2. (Vitaly Kuzmin)

THE INTERIOR TROOPS

The MVD also disposes of the Interior Troops (*Vnutrennye voiska*, VV), a substantial security force numbering some 140,000 officers and men. This is in effect a parallel "army," with military organization, ranks, and culture; it is distributed around the country, and is responsible primarily for public order and security, with a secondary disaster-relief function. The commander-in-chief of the VV also holds the appointment of deputy interior minister. He controls the force from Moscow, although operational command is exercised by the commanders of the seven VV MVD Districts, and local police chiefs (see accompanying panel).

The VV played a secondary but significant role in the First Chechen War (1994–96); in the initial year of the conflict, for example, 366 men were killed and 1,786 wounded. However, in many cases they were unenthusiastic; coordination with the regular military was poor, leading to a large number of "friendly-fire" incidents, and they often adopted a passive and reactive stance. Subsequent inquiries placed much of the blame for the rebels' recapture of Grozny in 1996 on the VVs' reluctance to launch aggressive patrols in and around the city, thus allowing the insurgents to mass in force away from the immediate environs of VV garrisons and checkpoints.

However, lessons were learned. After the initial assault they bore the brunt of the fighting during the Second Chechen War (1999–2009), since Moscow had recognized that the mechanized Russian Army, designed largely

Main Command   Central   North West

Volga   North Caucasus   Ural

Siberian   Far East   1st ODON

The sleeve insignia of the Interior Troops Districts and the 1st ODON. (Author's collection)

for conventional operations on the plains of Europe or Eurasia, was poorly prepared for counterinsurgency. To this end, the VV had by then received better training and equipment and, more to the point, adopted a more aggressive posture, which saw them using coordinated attacks, including artillery and air support, to take the war to the rebels. Although the latter had the advantage of local knowledge, a combination of war-weariness and internal divisions, coupled with the sheer size of the forces Russia was willing to deploy, meant that the insurgency was slowly ground down. By 2005, when Chechen rebel president Aslan Maskhadov was killed in a Russian attack, it was already on the wane.

VV forces vary considerably in size, effectiveness, and mission. They range from the elite *Spetsnaz* counterterrorist commando units of the various Special Purpose Detachments (*Otryady spetsialnogo naznacheniya*, OSNs), and the so-called "Dzerzhinsky Division" (1st ODON) garrisoning Moscow (both described below), through to local, relatively low-readiness units that are usually only employed in support of the police at sports fixtures and public events. Nonetheless, despite some suggestions in the 1990s that the force was a relic of Soviet authoritarianism that ought to be disbanded, the VV remains a key element of the Russian security forces. Although it has shrunk from its previous strength of 200,000, its future is not in doubt.

Men from the Interior Troops Central District assembling in the sidestreets around the Kremlin on the morning of the 2012 presidential elections; they wear *ushanka* hats rather than steel helmets, and have been issued batons. Note on their right sleeves the VV Central District's white-on-black falcon patch; these men are probably from either the 21st OBrON or the 95th Division. (Author's photo)

Organization

The Interior Troops are divided between a range of formations, each with slightly different roles and status. Most VV divisions are essentially just paper command structures, with the exception of the 1st Independent Special Purpose Division (*Otdelnaya diviziya osobennogo naznacheniya*, ODON).

The frontline elements of the VV are the Special Designation units, typically brigades or regiments. An Independent Special Purpose Brigade (*Otdelnaya brigada osobennogo naznacheniya*, OBrON) is a force of some 4,400 effectives, mainly motorized infantry, with around a third of its strength mechanized with BTR-80/80A armored personnel carriers; some serving in the North Caucasus have the newer, more heavily armed BTR-90 APCs and BMP-2 infantry fighting vehicles. Unlike the regular military, which is phasing-in Italian Fiat Iveco M65 light armored vehicles, the VV use only GAZ "Tigers." They are trained for a wide spectrum of missions, from counter-insurgency (many have been rotated through Chechnya and the other North Caucasian republics) to riot-control and maintenance of public order. The VV also has its own aviation branch, largely equipped with Mi-8 transport and assault helicopters and Mi-24P/V gunships, which saw extensive action in Chechnya. They wear military-pattern camouflage battledress and are equipped to Army light infantry standards, using AKS-74 and AKM-74 assault rifles, machine guns, RPG-22 and RPG-29 grenade-launchers, and other support weapons.

The bulk of the VV, however, are lower-status troops confined to guard and public-order duties. They are predominantly equipped as motorized infantry, but in practice spend much of their time as glorified static security guards. The 622nd VV Bn, for example, provides additional security for Moscow's Lefortovo prison, while the 620th VV Regt protects the Beloyarsk nuclear power station. The size of such units can vary considerably; while Moscow's elite 1st Independent Special Purpose Division is around 11,000 strong, the capital's 55th Division has an establishment strength closer to 6,500.

Interior Troops from Volga District (note the leaping deer sleeve patch) on parade in the city of Ufa. The berets are dark olive green, and bear a simple oval cockade badge. Note also the maroon-and-white striped *telnyashka* T-shirts, granted to the VV in an attempt to improve their *esprit de corps*. (Art Konovalov/Shutterstock.com)

There are also Special Motorized Police Battalions (*Spetsnialnye motorizovannye batalony politsii*, SMBP), modeled on Moscow's Operational Regiments. Technically part of the VV, they generally wear police uniforms and work most closely with local police commands, especially in providing additional manpower during times of particular need. These units are of no more than moderate quality; they are typically deployed in support of the police's own OMON – who are considered more skilled and determined – but they do provide quickly mobilized backup during disturbances or major public events.

Although the VV are equipped as light infantry their operational forces also include a few tank units (especially in 1st ODON), and some mechanized infantry mounted in BTR-80 and BTR-90 wheeled APCs and – as here – some BMP-2 infantry fighting vehicles, armed with 2A32 30mm cannon. (kojoku/Shutterstock.com)

25

The "Dzerzhinsky Division"

The 1st Independent Special Purpose Division (*1aya Otdelnaya diviziya osobennogo naznacheniya*, ODON) is a "Praetorian Guard" based in Moscow, with its own tank and artillery assets. Still widely known by its Soviet-era name of the "Dzerzhinsky Division," after the founder of Lenin's secret police, its history dates back to 1918, when the fledgling Bolshevik government formed the 1st Armored Car Squad to defend the leadership alongside the infamous Latvian riflemen who formed the core of their guards.

The MVD Interior Troops

Abbreviations: unit designation acronyms as in text and Glossary.
Also:

Bde = Brigade	Mar = Maritime
Bn = Battalion	MW = Mountain Warfare
Comms = Communications	Recon = Reconnaissance
Det = Detachment	Spec = Special
Div = Division	unident = unidentified
Ind = Independent	

Note: The order of the listing within each District, and the indenting of a few unit titles, follows the original Russian sources.

---

*Central VV MVD District
(HQ Moscow)*
1st Ind Spec Designation
  VV Div (Moscow)
604th Spec Purpose Center
  (Moscow)
95th VV Div (Moscow)
622nd Ind VV Bn (Moscow)
67th Ind VV Bn (Obolensk)
551st VV Regt (Moscow)
687th VV Regt (Moscow)
503rd VV Regt (Reutov)
unident Ind VV Bn (Dubna)
447th Ind VV Bn (Dubrovka)
164th Ind VV Bn (Desnogorsk)
165th Ind VV Bn (Udomlya)
21st OBrON (Sofrino)
unident Ind SMBP (Kostroma)
55th VV Div (Moscow)
102nd SMBP (Moscow)
104th SMBP (Moscow)
109th SMBP (Moscow)
107th SMBP (Moscow)
681st SMBP (Moscow)
547th SMBP (Elektrostal)
33rd VV OSN Peresvet (Moscow)
414th Ind SMBP (Yaroslavl)
unident Ind SMBP (Tver)

423rd Ind SMBP (Lyubertsy)
12th VV Div (Tula)
128th SMBP (Voronezh)
649th VV Regt (Bryansk)
597th SMBP (Kursk)
667th SMBP (Tula)
129th SMBP (Lipetsk)
591st VV Regt (Obninsk)
341st SMBP (Ivanovo)
518th SMBP (Vladimir)
426th Ind SMBP (Kaluga)
71st Ind VV Bn (Kurchatov)
unident Ind VV Bn
  (Novovoronezh)
683rd Ind VV Comm Regt
  (Moscow)
16th VV OSN Skif ("Scythian")
  (Rostov)
25th VV OSN Merkury
  (Zhornovka)

*Northwestern VV MVD District
(HQ St Petersburg)*
63rd OBrON (St Petersburg)
124th VV Regt (Sosnovy Bor)
2nd Marine VV Det (Murmansk)
33rd OBrON (Lebyazhye)
110th Ind SMBP (St Petersburg)

2nd SMBP (St Petersburg)
406th Ind SMBP (Kaliningrad)
614th VV Regt (Koryazhma)
418th Ind SMBP (Pankovka)
422nd Ind SMBP (Cherepovets)
420th Ind SMBP (Petrozavodsk)
421st Ind SMBP (Pskov)
28th VV OSN Ratnik
  ("Warrior") (Arkhangelsk)

*North Caucasian VV MVD
District (HQ Rostov)*
46th OBrON (Grozny)
424th OBrON (Grozny)
248th Ind Spec Mot VV Bn Sever
  ("North") (Grozny)
249th Ind Spec Mot VV Bn Yug
  ("South") (Vedeno)
140th VV Artillery Regt (Grozny)
34th VV OSN (Grozny)
358th Ind VV Bn (Shelkovsk)
94th VV Regt (Urus-Martan)
96th VV Regt (Gudermes)
352nd Ind VV Recon Bn (Grozny)
353rd Ind VV Comms Bn
  (Grozny)
360th Ind VV Bn (Shelkovskaya)
743rd Ind VV Bn (Vedeno)
744th Ind VV Bn (Nozhai-Yurt)
359th Ind SMBP (Grozny)
22nd OBrON (Kalach-na-Donu)
50th OBrON (Novocherkassk)
  7th VV OSN Rosich
  (Novocherkassk)
133rd SMBP (Novocherkassk)
2nd Ind Spec Designation VV Div
  (Krasnodar)
47th Ind VV Bde (Krasnodar)
  15th VV OSN Vyatich
  (Armavir)

From numbering fewer than 50 men, with two armored cars, some trucks mounting machine guns, and miscellaneous cars and motorcycles, this unit grew during the tumultuous era of the Russian Civil War (1918–21) until it numbered over a thousand men, including three infantry companies and a cavalry squadron. In 1921 it came under the control of the Cheka, the Bolshevik political police, and it remained part of that apparatus – in its successive incarnations – until the unit was transferred to the MVD after Stalin's death in 1953.

139th SMBP (Krasnodar)
127th SMBP (Sochi)
413th Ind SMBP (Elista)
378th Ind VV Bn (Labinsk)
215th Ind SMBP (Cherkessk)
346th Ind VV Recon Bn
  (Blagodarny)
49th Ind MW VV Bde
  (Vladikavkaz)
  unident Ind MW VV Bn
  (Nalchik)
  unident Ind MW VV Bn
  (Nazrak)
  unident Ind MW VV Bn
  (Kartsy)
383rd Ind VV Bn (Vladikavkaz)
121st VV Regt (Zvezdny)
674th VV Regt (Mozdok)
126th VV Regt (Nazran)
98th SMBP (Kislovodsk)
  17th VV OSN Edelveys
  (Mineralnye Vody)
362nd Ind VV Bn (Chermen)
372nd Ind VV Recon Bn
  (Zelenokumsk)
102nd OBrON (Makhachkala)
376th Ind VV Bn (Kizlyar)
450th Ind VV Bn (base unident)
375th Ind VV Bn (Astrakhan)
398th Ind VV Recon Bn
  (Astrakhan)

Volga VV MVD District
(HQ Nizhny Novgorod)
94th VV Div (Sarov)
43rd VV Regt (Sarov)
unident VV Regt (Sarov)
561st VV Regt (Dzerzhinsk)
34th OBrON
  (Nizhny Novgorod)
86th SMBP (Kazan)

26th VV OSN Bars ("Panther")
  (Kazan)
428th Ind VV Bn (Kazan)
79th VV Div (Kirov)
739th Ind SMBP (Izhevsk)
488th Ind SMBP (Gamovo)
379th Ind VV Bn (Zeleny)
419th Ind SMBP (Kirov)
unident SMBP (Ufa)
29th VV OSN Bulat (Ufa)
54th OBrON (Perm)
35th Ind VV Bde (Samara)
113th SMBP (Samara)
unident VV Regt (Tolyatti)
589th VV Regt (Zarechny)
738th Ind SMBP (Cheboksary)
unident SMBP (Volgograd)
20th VV OSN Viking
  (Saratov)

Ural VV MVD District
(HQ Yekaterinburg)
93rd VV Div (Chelyabinsk)
42nd VV Regt (Chelyabinsk)
545th VV Regt (Ozersk)
546th VV Regt (Tryekhgorny)
562nd VV Regt (Snezhinsk)
95th VV Regt (Kopeiisk)
23rd VV OSN Mechel
  (Chelyabinsk)
928th Ind VV Bn (Prezerny)
96th VV Div (Kalinovka-1)
543rd VV Regt (Novouralsk)
18th VV Regt (Nizhniy Tagil)
138th VV Regt (Lesnoi)
12th VV OSN Ural
  (Nizhniy Tagil)
620th VV Regt (Yekaterinburg)
395th Ind SMBP
  (Yekaterinburg)
131st SMBP (Persyabinsk)

Siberian VV MVD District
(HQ Novosibirsk)
19th VV OSN Ermak
  (Novosibirsk)
397th Ind SMBP (Novosibirsk)
98th VV Div (Kemerovo)
592nd VV Regt (Seversk)
41st VV Regt (Seversk)
555th VV Regt (Novosibirsk)
  27th VV OSN Kuzbass
  (Kemerovo)
82nd Ind VV Bde (Barnaul)
656th Operational Designation
  VV Regt (Rubtsovsk)
563rd VV Regt (Byysk)
42nd Ind VV Bde (Angarsk)
91st Ind VV Bde (Krasnoyarsk)
556th VV Regt (Krasnoyarsk)
557th VV Regt (Pogorny)
unident VV Regt (Zheleznogorsk)
407th Ind SMBP
  (Krasnoyarsk-45)

Eastern VV MVD District
(HQ Khabarovsk)
1st Mar VV Det (Khabarovsk)
21st VV OSN Taifun
  ("Typhoon") (Khabarovsk)
111th Ind VV Bde (Khabarovsk)
unident Ind SMBP (Khabarovsk)
107th Ind VV Bde (Vladivostok)
unident SMBP (Vladivostok)
24th VV OSN Svyatogor
  (Vladivostok)
388th Ind VV Bn (Elban)
374th Ind VV Bn (Chuguevka)
150th Ind SMBP (Yuzhno-
  Sakhalinsk)
unident VV Regt (Magadan)

An armored-vehicle crewman from the VV 1st Independent Special Purpose Division (1 ODON). Note the white-metal collar badge of the VV; the division's panther patch on his right sleeve (white-on-black, with a yellow edge); and, just visible on his left sleeve (see also Plate C, inset 2a), the red, white, and yellow Interior Troops patch. (Vitaly Kuzmin)

Its primary role remained the protection of the Kremlin and the senior Communist Party leadership, but it also acted as an elite military strike force for the suppression of resistance to the state. In the 1920s and 1930s, for example, detachments from what had then become a division-strength force were involved in suppressing peasant risings in the Ukraine, and fighting against the *basmachi* rebels of Central Asia. During World War II the division participated in the defense of Moscow in 1942, and later in the extermination of Ukrainian nationalist partisans.[2]

In 1953 the Dzerzhinsky Division moved across to the MVD, becoming a factor in Moscow's military balance of power. The KGB (as the political police became known in 1954) had the Kremlin Guard; the regular Army, the 2nd Guards Tamanskaya Motor Rifle Division and 4th Guards Kantemirovskaya Tank Division; and the MVD, the Dzerzhinsky Division. In 1977, out of concern that the 1980 Moscow Olympics might attract an attack, a specialized antiterrorist unit was formed within the division; in 1989 this Special Purpose Company (RSN) would become Vityaz, discussed below. The 1980s were turbulent years for the decaying USSR, and the division had to send detachments to deal with crises across the country, from the aftermath of the 1986 Chernobyl nuclear disaster to taking part in crackdowns in Tbilisi, Georgia, in 1989 and Baku, Azerbaijan, in 1990.

The division has a reputation for rigid adherence to orders. During the short-lived August 1991 coup in which hard-liners sought in vain to reverse Soviet President Mikhail Gorbachev's liberalizing reforms, it obeyed Interior Minister Boriss Pugo, who was one of the plotters, and was almost deployed against the crowds supporting opposition leader Boris Yeltsin. Conversely, after the end of the USSR, in 1993 the division had no qualms in obeying Yeltsin's orders to assist in the violent dissolution of a Communist-dominated parliament. In 1994 it was renamed the

2 See MAA 412, *Ukrainian Armies 1914–1955*

Independent Special Purpose Division (or technically, the even more cumbersome "Independent Special Purpose, Orders of Lenin and the October Revolution, Red Banner Division," reflecting its past battle honors), and also acquired its current insignia of a panther. It has sent troops to Chechnya and other Caucasus flashpoints, as well as carrying out public-order duties in Moscow.

As an MVD unit, the 1st ODON escaped the reductions from division to brigade strength which took place within the regular Army. It is unusually large for a VV division, with some 11,000 men – although at its peak in the 1980s and 1990s it numbered almost 18,000 – and currently comprises four motor rifle (mechanized) regiments, a smaller special motorized police regiment (whose members wear police rather than VV uniforms), an artillery battalion, an engineer battalion, a chemical and biological protection battalion, a firefighting battalion, a field hospital, a Commandant's Service military police company, and associated specialist, training, and logistics elements. It is based at a sprawling complex in Moscow's eastern Balashikha suburb, with an additional training facility at Noginsk further to the east along the Vladimir road. The majority of its officers and men are professionals, but it is presently anticipated that it will continue to take some conscripts – typically, the pick of the draft pool – until at least 2018.

VV *Spetsnaz*

The VV also disposes of a number of *spetsnaz* special-purpose detachments (*Otryady spetsialnogo naznacheniya*, OSN). In the Russian military lexicon the term "detachment" implies no fixed size or organization, and OSNs range from 30-man platoons up to the Central District's reinforced-company Peresvet unit based in Moscow. Each VV District has at least one OSN attached to it, largely responsible for counterterrorist operations but also occasionally detailed to support the police in extreme cases.

Soldiers of the Moscow-based 33rd VV Special Purpose Detachment (OSN), named "Peresvet" after a medieval Russian hero who fell fighting the Mongols. They have AK-74 assault rifles with blank-firing attachments on the muzzles, and a couple also carry holstered Makarov pistols. Their camouflage fatigues incorporate areas of both four-color stipple pattern and plain drab – see also the close-up photo on page 60. (Vitaly Kuzmin)

Each OSN has its own name and distinctive symbol, in part as a way of strengthening *esprit de corps*, since almost all are creations of the post-Soviet era and thus lack unit traditions. Nonetheless, they enjoy an exalted status within the VV. One of the USSR's first specialized antiterrorist units was the Dzerzhinsky Division's Special Purpose Company, later renamed the 6th VV OSN Vityaz ("Knight"). It was joined in 1994 by a sister unit, Rus', and both saw considerable action in Chechnya. In 2008 both were transferred out of the division to form the MVD's 604th Special Purpose Center (*Tsentr*

Unarmed combat is central to the training of Russian special and security forces. Here, troopers of the 33rd VV OSN Peresvet engage in a demonstration of "Sambo," a martial art developed specifically for Soviet troops as early as the 1920s. Its name derives from a contraction of *samooborona bez oruzhiya,* "self-defense without weapons."(Vitaly Kuzmin)

spetsialnogo naznacheniya, TsSN), a counterterrorism force under the direct control of the central ministry apparatus. As such, it works with the Central Region TsN but is not ultimately subordinated to it.

VV *Spetsnaz* are specially trained in small-unit operations, especially hostage rescues, forced entries, and detaining or eliminating armed suspects. Some units also have particular forms of expertise. For example, Edelveys ("Edelweiss"), the 17th VV OSN based in the southern upland town of Mineralnye Vody, is known for its mountain-warfare skills. Likewise, the 28th VV OSN Ratnik, "Warrior" from the northern port city of Arkhangelsk, has experience in Arctic operations. All recruits receive rigorous physical training in unarmed and armed combat, and develop specialities such as sniper, scout, and negotiator skills. Many of these units have also rotated

C · INTERIOR TROOPS

(1) Sniper, 28th Special Purpose Detachment; Northwestern District, 2011

The Interior Troops' experiences in Chechnya left them with an appreciation of snipers and the need to counter them. One response was the 12.7mm OSV-96 anti-material rifle, a massive beast with a maximum effective range of over 1,800m (more than a mile) against large targets. In practice, this very heavy weapon is unpopular, not least because of a tendency of its PSO sight to work loose. This sniper from 28 VV OSN Ratnik ("Warrior"), based in Arkhangelsk, has tucked a PYa pistol into a pocket of his Chameleon sniper's vest as a back-up weapon. He is a highly qualified "red beret," although in action he would probably replace this with less conspicuous headgear. His SPOSN SS-Leto ("SS-summer") camouflage fatigues bear no distinguishing insignia, but note the maroon-and-white VV version of the *telnyashka* that he is wearing beneath the jacket.

(2) Sergeant, 1st ODON; Moscow, 2012

This sergeant from the VV 1st Independent Specialized Purpose Division is pictured at leisure on a Moscow street. His rank is shown by the three subdued-tone green stripes across the epaulets of his digital Flora pattern camouflage fatigues, and his formation by the ODON's panther patch on his right sleeve. Though it is obscured here, he would be wearing the full-color VV patch on his left sleeve **(inset 2a)**. Unusually, he is wearing the regular MVD police cockade badge on his field cap: perhaps he is relying on the left-pocket pin indicating past service in Chechnya to deflect the ire of any senior officer spotting this minor military faux pas.

(3) Private, 34th Independent Special Purpose Brigade; Volga District, 2011

34 OBrON is an Interior Troops rapid-readiness unit. This soldier wears standard digital Flora camouflage battledress, with the subdued version of the VV badge on his left sleeve; the deer stenciled on the side of his 6B7-1M helmet is the symbol of the Volga District Interior Troops. He is heavily laden, with a 6B12 armored vest and an Ataka-2 rucksack with sleeping bag and bedroll. Note that he has one of the new AN-94 Abakan assault rifles; since 34 OBrON has not been generally issued this weapon, he is probably engaged in a round of technical evaluations.

1

2a

2

3

through Chechnya, both to acquire combat experience and to provide a sharper edge to the existing VV forces deployed there. The only exception is Peresvet, which is always kept in Moscow in case of emergencies in the capital.

Red-beret personnel

The true "elite within an elite" will have gone through the grueling tests that can lead to the award of the prized red beret (actually, closer to maroon in color). Award of the red beret is on an individual basis, distinct from membership of any particular unit; the more genuinely elite units will typically be largely or wholly made up of "red berets," but for even half of a unit's personnel to enjoy this status is impressive.

The test is divided into three main stages, which are run with minimal opportunity for rest in between. The first is a test of fitness and stamina, with candidates required to run an 8km (5-mile) cross-country race followed by a sprint, under exceedingly arduous conditions (including fording deep water, crossing an obstacle course, and running through a simulated contamination zone while wearing a gas mask). Meanwhile, instructors will be trying to distract the candidates with everything from verbal abuse to pyrotechnics. The second stage is a test of marksmanship with a variety of weapons, concluding in a simulated hostage rescue in which the candidate must "double tap" two targets representing hostiles without harming the target representing their captive. The final test is of unarmed combat skills; in four 3-minute rounds, the candidate will face four separate, fresh assailants, all "red beret" experts. The rules are brutally simple: no blows to the groin, spine, elbows or knees, but beyond that everything is fair game, and broken bones and concussion are not unusual. All the candidate has to do is make it through these 12 minutes conscious and mobile, but most find this the most demanding stage of all. Less than half the candidates succeed in passing all three stages with flying colors, and it is not unusual to find men retaking them several years in succession before finally qualifying.

Chechen MVD forces: the "*Kadyrovtsy*"

In order successfully to combat the Chechen resistance Moscow eventually had to rely on local auxiliaries, who came to dominate the republic. Former rebel Akhmad Kadyrov, who was effectively the Chechen leader from 2000 (although he was only elected president in 2003), started this process, taking over the Grozny OMON and granting his personal guard the status of a government security force. When he was assassinated by rebels in 2004, his fiery son Ramzan became increasingly powerful, and assumed the presidency in 2007. Ramzan Kadyrov, having led his father's private militia, essentially turned the republican security forces into his personal retinue. In 2004 his father's bodyguards were formally made part of the Chechen Republic MVD, and by 2006 the so-called *Kadyrovtsy* ("Kadyrovites") dominated the local security apparatus. Although they were officially rolled into the local MVD structures, they were personally loyal to the younger Kadyrov rather than to Moscow. At that point they numbered over 5,000 men in two MVD units – the 141st "Akhmad Kadyrov" Special Purpose Police Regiment (also sometimes called PPSM-2), and the Oil Regiment (*Neftepolk*), formally tasked with guarding local pipelines – as well as several still-unofficial ex-guerrilla units euphemistically described as Anti-Terrorism Centers. The latter were inducted into the MVD as the Sever ("North") and Yug ("South") battalions.

The Yamadayev brothers

Although Moscow was happy to pass a growing share of the counterinsurgency burden to the Chechens, who as a force of "turned" ex-guerrillas were best able to take on the rebels on their own terms, it was not especially comfortable with the autonomy that the volatile Ramzan Kadyrov had acquired. One response was to try to maintain alternative Chechen forces as counterweights, largely by supporting in parallel the Yamadayev brothers. These were also former rebel commanders who had switched sides to the Russians. Two special units had been founded by the GRU (Military Intelligence) in 1999: the Vostok ("East") and Zapad ("West") battalions. Also made up of former rebels, these were kept apart from the Chechen MVD and subordinated instead to the Russian Army.

However, enemies of the Kadyrovs rarely seem to prosper. Dzhabrail Yamadayev, commander of the Vostok Bn, was killed by an unexplained bomb attack in 2003, after which his brother Sulim took over the unit. A third brother, Ruslan, was murdered in Moscow in 2008 while in Sulim's car; Sulim blamed Kadyrov's agents for being behind the attack. After gunmen from the Vostok Bn and the *Kadyrovtsy* clashed outside the Chechen town of Gudermes, leaving 18 dead, Ramzan successfully demanded that Sulim Yamadayev be dismissed. He fled to Dubai, where he was murdered in 2009; the local police accused a cousin of Kadyrov's of the killing.

Ramzan Kadyrov, the volatile leader of the Chechen Republic government; he renounced the title of "president" in 2010, saying that Russia should have only one of those. His seemingly unquestioned authority in Chechnya depends in part on Moscow's support, but also reflects his personal control of the republic's extensive security apparatus. (zmax/Shutterstock.com)

With the demise of the Yamadayevs, Kadyrov's control over Chechen forces became unchallenged. The Vostok and Zapad units, which had largely stayed out of the political fray, were disbanded at the end of 2008, although the former had just fought in Georgia during Russia's three-day invasion of that country. Meanwhile, the *Kadyrovtsy* have been equipped to regular OMON and VV standard, though their discipline is often questionable, and they have been accused of numerous human-rights abuses by international observers. Nonetheless, their ferocity has never been in doubt, and they have been successful in grinding away at the resolve and numbers of the remaining insurgents. At the time of writing, although there are still sporadic terrorist attacks in Chechnya, the days of a sizable, coherent insurgent force that could challenge the authorities for control of territory are over.

The Lubyanka building, once the nerve center of the KGB, on Moscow's Dzerzhinzsky Square (named after the first chief of the Bolshevik secret police). Its looming presence in fact distracts attention from the real headquarters of the KGB's successor, the Federal Security Service, which is situated in the gray block to the left, at No. 1 Bolshaya Lubyanka Street. The Lubyanka itself now accommodates the headquarters of the FSB Border Troops and several administrative departments. (Author's photo)

THE FEDERAL SECURITY SERVICE (FSB)

The Federal Security Service (*Federalnaya sluzhba bezopasnosti*, FSB) is the main internal security agency, and President Putin's own former service – he was its director in 1998–99. It emerged from a prolonged period of transition within the security apparatus following the ostensible disbandment of the infamous Soviet KGB (Committee of State Security) in 1991. In fact, most of the KGB's domestic security elements within what was to become the Russian Federation were incorporated into a Russian successor agency, briefly called the Federal Security Agency (1991–92), then the Ministry of Security (1992–94), before becoming the Federal Counterintelligence Service (FSK). In 1995 this was finally rechristened the FSB.

The service endured periods of political suspicion and budgetary constraints in the 1990s that led to increasing corruption and a hemorrhage of able officers. Only under Putin did it regain its previous privileged status and an *esprit de corps* that explicitly draws on the traditions of the KGB. Under Putin it has become increasingly powerful, and to some extent this is reflected in the status and number of its militarized forces. The FSB has a variety of special security elements at its disposal. The key ones are Alpha and Vympel, but each district has its own SOBR-type unit, such as Grad ("Hail") for the St Petersburg city and regional FSB Directorate, and another in Yessentuki for the southern region.

ALPHA

Russia's senior antiterrorism commando unit, which has been deployed at all key events of recent years, is the FSB's Alpha (*Al'fa*) group. Although other units tend to question whether it is any more skilled and professional than they are, it is undoubtedly the most famous of Russia's security forces, and enjoys a reputation for ruthless proficiency.

It was formed within the KGB's Seventh (Surveillance) Directorate in 1974, and, like the Dzerzhinsky Division's RSN, this was initially a response to the approach of the 1980 Moscow Olympics. Following the Munich massacre at the 1972 Olympics in Germany, when Palestinians killed 11 Israeli athletes and officials and a West German police officer, KGB chairman Yuri Andropov wanted to ensure that the USSR had a counterterrorist force comparable to West

An operator from the Interior Troops' 604th Special Purpose Center, one of the most elite of the *spetsgruppy*. Black tactical uniforms and masked balaclavas have become commonplace among such units, leading some other police officers to describe them collectively as "black masks." Although the FSB's Alpha remains Russia's most celebrated antiterrorist outfit, the gap in training, capability, and kit between it and units such as the 604th TsSN is narrowing. (Vitaly Kuzmin)

Germany's GSG-9 and Britain's SAS. Originally numbering 30 men under Col Vitaly Bubenin, it attracted military *Spetsnaz*, athletes, and even one USSR boxing champion, Gleb Tolstikov. It grew steadily to just under 100 men by 1979, with smaller detachments based in Alma-Ata, Khabarovsk, Kiev, Krasnodar, Minsk, and Sverdlovsk (the city later renamed Yekaterinburg), to ensure a rapid response to any incidents. Alpha saw its first taste of action in an unexpected and offensive role, however.

As the Soviets prepared their invasion of Afghanistan in 1979 – hoping to pacify the country quickly with a show of force, and to replace the radical Communist leader Hafizullah Amin with the more tractable Babrak Karmal – two detachments each of 24 Alpha operators, codenamed Grom ("Thunder") and Zenit ("Zenith"), were secretly infiltrated to Kabul. They were led by Viktor Karpukhin, who would later command Alpha and who remains a legendary figure amongst the *Spetsnaz*. On December 27, 1979, along with military *Spetsnaz* and paratroopers, they launched Operation Storm-333, seizing the presidential Tajbeg Palace and killing Amin. Alpha lost only two soldiers in the attack despite the heavy defenses around the palace. Thereafter Alpha would play a sporadic role in the ensuing Afghan War (1979–89), but its primary role remained domestic.[3]

The Moscow Olympics passed without incident (beyond the Western boycott in protest at the Soviet invasion of Afghanistan), but in the years to come Alpha would be called upon to respond to a range of difficult challenges. For example, in Sarapul in 1981 two draftees took 25 children hostage at a local school and demanded to be flown to the West. Both were seized after a period of negotiation, with all the hostages released unharmed. More bloody was the hijacking of an Aeroflot passenger jet on a domestic flight in 1983. The hijackers, seven young Georgians, were demanding to be allowed to fly to Turkey. Instead the aircraft landed at the Georgian capital, Tbilisi, and negotiations began. On the second day of the siege Alpha commandos stormed the plane. Three hijackers were killed and the other four arrested,

3 See MAA 178, *Russia's War in Afghanistan*

The retired MajGen Gennady Zaitsev (right), a legendary figure within the Russian special forces community, is a former commander of Alpha. Here he is shown with Col Viktor Dezhurov, head of the Federal Penitentiary Service (FSIN) Moscow directorate, presenting awards to the winners in an interagency contest organized in 2011 to mark the 19th anniversary of the founding of the FSIN's Saturn team. Zaitsev wears a general's gray tunic, with the red-ribboned Hero of the Soviet Union star pinned above his lesser decorations. Dezhurov wears the dark blue FSIN uniform. (Vitaly Kuzmin)

but the dead also included three crew members and two passengers. The internal report on the incident has never been released, but there have been persistent claims that Alpha put a higher priority on taking down the hijackers than on protecting the hostages.

During the dying days of the Soviet Union, Alpha's notoriety increased when it was involved in violent clashes with Azeri nationalists in January 1990; and with Lithuanian protesters in January 1991 (in which one member of the group died in the crossfire). When hard-line Communists launched their coup against Soviet President Gorbachev in August 1991, and Russian President Yeltsin became the focus for resistance, MajGen Karpukhin, who had risen to become commander of Alpha, was tasked by the conspirators with storming the Russian parliament building known as the White House and arresting Yeltsin. Karpukhin, who was known for leading from the front, mingled with the crowds of protesters around the White House to reconnoiter the potential operation. He concluded that, while the mission was feasible, it would entail heavy civilian casualties, and he conveyed this to the coup leaders. Ultimately, the order for the assault was never given, not least because of the reservations of Karpukhin and others. Within three days the coup had collapsed, one of the deciding factors being the plotters' failure to seize Yeltsin, whose defiant speech to the crowd from the top of an APC was an image that traveled round the world.

Karpukhin was dismissed, and Alpha, under LtCol Mikhail Golovatov, was made directly subordinate to Yeltsin. By this time it had expanded to a Moscow unit of 200 operators and another 300 divided between the regional units. However, any gratitude Yeltsin may have felt toward Alpha was short-lived. In the period 1991–92, as the value of the ruble plummeted, he raised the salaries of Alpha officers ten-fold, but this did not buy their complete acquiescence. In October 1993, Yeltsin decided to dissolve his unruly parliament. He called on Alpha (ironically enough) to carry out the same mission that it had been reluctant to undertake in 1991: storming the White House. The unit's

FEDERAL SECURITY SERVICE

D

(1) Private, Border Troops; Russian Far East, 2009
Typical equipment for a Border Troops soldier surveying a sector of the Chinese frontier might be these TBP-2 high-powered binoculars mounted on a Soviet-vintage tripod. He carries a slung AK-74 rifle. Over his winter-weight field uniform he is wearing a camouflage oversuit in the Klyaksa ("ink blots") pattern, and he has a black woolen cap instead of the usual fleece-flapped *ushanka*.

(2) Alpha commando; Beslan, 2004
This Alpha sniper is keeping the school at Beslan under observation through the PSO-1 scope of his VSS Vintorez silenced sniper rifle. His Altyn helmet includes a communications connection; it also has the optional armored visor, which offers protection at the cost of weight and discomfort, as well as limiting the wearer's vision and hearing. It is often therefore left off, or replaced with a

clear plastic shield, by troops engaging in a direct assault. He wears Partizan camouflage fatigues, under a 6B5-19 vest with a titanium breastplate. The white armband is for friend-or-foe identification in situations in which the enemy may be wearing Russian battledress, as was the case at Beslan.

(3) FSB officer; Kaliningrad, 2007
This plainclothes officer from the Economic Security Directorate of the Federal Security Service is taking part in a raid on a gang of smugglers in Kaliningrad. He is tugging from a sports bag a Kazak-4 vest with "FSB" markings, for both protection and recognition purposes, while trying to cover the area with his Makarov PMM pistol. Although dated, the PMM it is still favored by many undercover officers; so many are in circulation on the black market that it does not identify the bearer as a government agent in the way that possession of a more modern weapon might.

1

3

2

ФСБ

commanders made their lack of enthusiasm obvious, but did agree to scout out the area and open talks with its defenders in a bid to persuade them to surrender.

The circumstances are unclear, but some of the defenders opened fire on a group of soldiers close to the White House. When Alpha commandos began helping evacuate the wounded, an operator named Gennady Sergeyev was shot and killed by a sniper. This stiffened their resolve; they took the lead in the operation that saw the White House shelled into submission, but Yeltsin would not forget their earlier qualms. Alpha was briefly slated to be subordinated to the MVD, in what would have been a clear demotion, but in 1995 it became part of the FSB instead, as Directorate A of the FSB Special Purpose Center (TsSN FSB). It grew to a strength of 720, with just under 400 operators and around 320 support staff, and regional bases at Yekaterinburg, Krasnodar, and Khabarovsk.

The Dubrovka Theater
The unit played a significant role in both Chechen wars, especially in operations to kill or capture rebel commanders. However, their main role would be in responding to a number of high-profile terrorist and insurgent operations, most notably at Budyonnovsk (Budenovsk) in 1995, Pervomaiskoye in 1996, the Dubrovka Theater in Moscow in 2002, and the Beslan school siege in 2004. In the process it acquired a reputation both for expertise and inventiveness, and also for a sometimes heavy-handed approach.

In October 2002, for example, about 40 Chechen terrorists seized the Dubrovka Theater in Moscow during a performance, taking 850 hostages. They demanded an immediate ceasefire in Chechnya followed by a full Russian withdrawal. It is unclear whether they genuinely believed there was any chance that the Kremlin would accede to these unrealistic demands. A two-and-a-half-day standoff ensued, punctuated by abortive efforts at negotiations, the release of some hostages, and some fatal and non-fatal clashes (including a grenade attack that injured two Alpha officers who were reconnoitering the outside of the building).

Early on the morning of the third day, the security forces began pumping fentanyl gas into the building through its ventilation system. This powerful narcotic allowed commandos from Alpha, supported by the separate FSB Vympel force and the Moscow SOBR, to storm the booby-trapped building without the heavily armed terrorists being able to massacre the hostages. Thirty-nine terrorists died (reports are inconclusive as to whether any managed to escape); in some cases, based on their wounds, they may have been shot in the head while already unconscious. However, the concentrations of gas were such that 178 of the 179 hostages who also died were killed by its effects, and only one by hostile fire. These problems were compounded by delays in evacuating them from the theater, and in passing details of the gas to the medical teams present.

While the methods used to lift the Dubrovka Theater siege caused controversy internationally and among activists and bereaved relatives at home, opinion polls showed that most Russians supported them. The operation exemplified Alpha's approach, characterized by creativity and the rapid application of overwhelming and precise firepower, but also by a disregard for certain niceties that their Western counterparts would be expected to observe. In this case the protection of civilians proved a less absolute objective than eliminating the terrorists, and Alpha have distinctly permissive guidelines for the use of deadly force against targets.

Training and equipment

Alpha operators are recruited from the military, MVD, FSB, and other militarized services or military academies, usually through a recommendation by a serving *Spetsnaz* officer. All are volunteers, almost all holding officer ranks (there are a few NCOs in driving, training, and logistical positions). The upper age limit for new recruits is 28, although once within Alpha soldiers may serve for as long as they continue to meet fitness and other standards, and it has been known for this age limit to be relaxed when experienced *Spetsnaz* from other units are transferring across to Alpha. Applicants must be extremely fit, at least 175cm tall (5ft 9in), and must pass the usual barrage of medical, physical, and psychological tests. Each must also pass a background and character check comparable to that faced by regular FSB security officers (in Western terms, this is equivalent to being cleared to access Secret materials). While Alpha operators – like so many Russian soldiers – have a reputation as recreational drinkers, any suggestion of a dependence on drugs or alcohol will disbar a candidate. Interestingly enough, a criminal record is not in itself enough to exclude an otherwise suitable recruit, although breaking the law once within the unit is regarded very seriously.

Training is extensive, and comparable in many ways to that undergone by similar counterterrorist forces around the world. Generally, recruits go through a standard one-year program that covers everything from basic marksmanship to parachuting; they are then assigned to parent units on a probationary basis, still under training, especially in technical specializations. It will generally take another 3–4 years before they are put forward for full graduation, passing through an ordeal analogous to that faced by would-be VV "red berets." Again, those with extensive prior experience may be allowed to move more quickly through the program.

Alpha's main base and training center are at Balashikha on the east of Moscow, but recruits spend considerable time familiarizing themselves with operations in other climates; this reflects their role as the final resource for serious terrorist or criminal threats anywhere in this vast country. In particular, Alpha also uses the FSB's special training facility outside Makhachkala in Dagestan, where operators train for potential deployments

The specialized Abaim-Abanat assault vehicle. Based on a GAZ-233034 "Tiger" armored car, this is used to quickly establish an entry point in an elevated location such as a hijacked airliner or the upper floor of a building. Note the armored shield with vision port at the end of the "cherry-picker" extendable ramp; generally in an assault a squad will shelter behind the vehicle while one man takes point behind the shield. (Vitaly Kuzmin)

to the North Caucasus; they use it as a base from which to launch mountain operations, and familiarize themselves with key cities in the region. They may also use the MVD's 8th Special Purpose Mountain Training Center at Khatsavita in the nearby Krasnodar region. Like any special forces, Alpha train constantly, even after graduation, and some also go on to study advanced intelligence tradecraft at the FSB Academy in southwest Moscow or the training schools of other Russian security agencies.

As befits such an elite unit, Alpha's operators have their pick of weapons and equipment, which increasingly include specially imported items from abroad. Although their specific load-out will depend entirely on the nature and duration of their mission, their primary weapons are AKM-74 assault rifles, as well as some of the new AN-94 Abakans, AKS-74U and AK-105 assault carbines, and PP-19 and 9A-91 SMGs. Although they may use Makarov PMM or PYa Grach pistols, most prefer Western Glocks and similar advanced handguns. Unlike the "snipers" of the regular VV, who are essentially regular infantry with a little extra marksmanship training, Alphas train extensively and so merit high-precision weapons. Although some Russian SV-98 sniper rifles are in service, most Alpha sharpshooters use the British Accuracy International AWM-F chambered in .338 Lapua Magnum, with Zeiss 3-12×56 SSG series telescopic sights. For specific missions they also use a range of silenced weapons, including the PSS pistol, AS Val carbine, and VSS sniper rifle.

In full combat conditions they will also use whatever heavier weapons they think necessary, including RPG rocket-launchers, GP-25 and GP-30 under-barrel grenade-launchers, and RPO-A Schmel incendiary-rocket launchers. They have deployed in a range of vehicles, from BTR-series armored personnel carriers and BMP infantry fighting vehicles through to nondescript trucks and cars, and, for surprise raids, even in regular commercial vans converted with internal armor and bulletproof glass.

A monument in Ulyanovsk to LtCol Dmitry Razumovsky, commander of the Vympel assault unit during the 2004 Beslan school massacre. He fell in the attack, and was posthumously made a Hero of the Russian Federation for his efforts to save the hostages being held by Chechen terrorists. (ppl/Shutterstock.com)

VYMPEL

Vympel ("Pennant") is now a specialized antiterrorist and, in particular, a nuclear-security force. In contrast to Alpha, which was originally intended as a defensive counterterrorist force but was pressed into service in more offensive roles, Vympel was established from the start for much more aggressive missions.

It was formed in 1981 within the KGB's First Chief Directorate (responsible for overseas espionage) on the basis of 25 men from Zenit ("Zenith"), one of the Alpha subunits that had taken part in Operation Storm-333 in 1979 (see above). By contrast with Alpha, Vympel was intended for missions abroad, including covert surveillance, hostage-rescue, assassination, and

Operators from Vympel, part of the FSB's Special Purpose Center. Note the commercially purchased Petzl harness over the left man's tactical vest, and the Yarygin PYa pistol in his shoulder holster. His left hand is gloved to allow him to use it for braking while rappelling down a building, while his right hand is ungloved to allow maximum dexterity for shooting. (Vitaly Kuzmin)

sabotage. Its operators therefore had to master foreign languages (the minimum requirement was fluency in one and a basic knowledge of a second), and various means of deployment, from HALO parachute insertion to traveling commercially under false identities. Of course, this was not at the expense of combat and physical training, including proficiency with a wide range of the foreign weapons that they might encounter when operating abroad. Given the range of skills they were expected to master, it took five years fully to train a Vympel *Spetsnaz* officer even though most already had KGB or military experience, but nevertheless the unit's strength steadily increased.

Vympel deployed to Afghanistan in the 1980s (losing only one member throughout the whole war), and when the KGB was formally dissolved in 1991 it was transferred to the new Russian security structure. However, in 1993 it went even further than Alpha, and flatly refused President Yeltsin's orders to storm the White House. As a result it was punished by a transfer from the Ministry of Security to the MVD. This was not just a symbolic demotion; it also meant that its members' salaries were cut, and their duties changed to policing work. The result was disastrous: of its 500 personnel, 320 moved to other units, 120 simply left government service (including most of the frontline operators), and only around 50 accepted this transfer.

The MVD made the best of the situation, renaming the unit Vega and seeking to recruit extra operators, but at this time the ministry lacked the prestige and the resources to compete either with other comparable agencies (Alpha, after all, was expanding), or with the private security industry. Vega never really emerged as a viable unit. However, in 1994 the FSK, successor to the Security Ministry, established its Special Purpose Center under Gen Dmitry Gerasimov, who had formerly headed Vympel. He was keen to "rescue" his old service, and in 1995 it was transferred back to the Security Service, now called the FSB. There it regained its old name (although it was originally called Directorate V of the Directorate for the Defense of the Constitution and Combating Terrorism), and was subordinated to the new TsSN in a counterterrorism role alongside Alpha.

Vympel essentially shares Alpha's uniforms and equipment, and to a considerable extent it also has the same recruitment criteria and training. However, reflecting its pedigree, it specializes in covert surveillance and insertion operations, and therefore emphasizes training in parachuting, maritime, and underwater deployment, and urban and mountain combat. In light of this skill set it was inevitable that Vympel would be used in Chechnya, where, like Alpha, it tended to be deployed specifically to seize or eliminate rebel commanders. In 2000, for example, a Vympel team snatched the rebel warlord Salman Raduyev in the town of Novogroznensky following a tip-off. This was a particular coup for Vympel, since at that time Raduyev, organizer of the 1996 Kizlyar raid into neighboring Dagestan, was considered Russia's second most wanted man. Not all their operations went so well, however. In April 2005 a run-of-the-mill raid on five terrorists in an apartment in Grozny went bad, and five Vympel operators were killed in the firefight. However, the unit's single greatest loss of life was suffered at the 2004 Beslan siege (see above), where seven men died including the commanding officer.

"Tiger" teams

Vympel is also designated the lead agency to respond to threats of nuclear terrorism or proliferation, and still regularly mounts "tiger team" exercises to test the readiness and effectiveness of guards at nuclear sites and on convoys. Its relations with the soldiers of the 12th Main Directorate of the Defense Ministry, who are primarily responsible for these nuclear security duties, tends to be competitive at best, hostile at worst.

These exercises are often complex and lengthy, reflecting Vympel's motto: "Timing, Thoroughness and Reliability." In 1999, for example, Vympel took part in the Arzamas-16 exercise in the "closed city" of Sarov, home of Russia's nuclear bomb. First it carried out a long-term operation to establish a base of operations in the city and a route by which to bring in its officers without alerting the FSB teams monitoring the city or the MVD forces controlling access by road and rail. Eventually they set up a small travel agency and tourist bureau, and developed a plan to smuggle additional men in underwater via the nearby Satis River. They then infiltrated the city from a staging post 30km (19 miles) away, past MVD patrols and watch stations, and simulated an attack on the Avangard warhead facility. Alpha and some 5,000 police were involved in further exercises based on resisting such an attack, and retaking a train captured by terrorists. In 2007, another series of exercises in the Urals Chelyabinsk region saw Vympel operators playing the part of the terrorists; they managed to breach security at the Trechgorny nuclear site, and seized hostages and a simulated nuclear device on a train.

BORDER TROOPS

Since 2003 the FSB has also controlled the Federal Border Service. This agency, in turn, controls the Border Troops (*Pogranichnye voiska*, PV), whose 175,000 male and female personnel include not only the unarmed officers scrutinizing passports at Russia's airports, but also a militarized border security force. Recognizable by the distinctive green trim to their caps, badges, and shoulder boards, the PV have a long tradition of serious military operations. Their predecessors were the first to fight Napoleon's invading armies in 1812; they faced Hitler's onslaught in World War II (some 150 were made Heroes of the Soviet Union, many posthumously); and they bore the brunt of clashes with the Chinese over the Ussuri River in 1969.[4]

In post-Soviet times they are responsible for what are still the longest land borders in the world, including such troublesome stretches as the North Caucasus frontier, and they have also been involved in efforts to control the cross-border movement of insurgents in Central Asia and of heroin from Afghanistan. Between 1993 and 2005 the Russian PV were deployed in Tajikistan to help guard the border with Afghanistan until local forces were deemed to be up to the task.

The PV are organized into Border Districts (*Pogranichnye okrugy*, PO): the Central, Northwest, Southern, Ural, Volga, Siberian, Far Eastern, and Arctic Districts. These mirror the country's Federal Districts apart from the Arctic PO, which is essentially a Maritime Border Guard command. POs have their own mobile groups, which are largely motorized patrol forces but supported by heli-mobile elements, and company-strength "special purpose" units that, despite their name, should not be considered comparable to the other *Spetsnaz* forces. Instead, these are rapid-response motorized detachments deployed in cases of higher-intensity operations, such as interdicting drug and gun caravans or supporting regular PVs. However, as each PO has different challenges, the size and nature of their forces vary considerably. The Central PO only borders Belarus, for example, and thus is largely concerned with monitoring land and air transport. By contrast, the Southern PO is the most militarized, since it includes the North Caucasus and is responsible for interdicting movements by insurgents and their supplies.

The Border Troops also have less conventional challenges. In the Caspian Sea, for example, PV maritime patrols deploy patrol boats and helicopters against caviar poachers, who are often armed and who use small, fast, very shallow-draft boats with considerable maneuverability. The Far Eastern and Ural POs cover especially long stretches of border with China, Kazakhstan, and Mongolia; these commands therefore have extensive air assets, including Mi-24P/V "Hind" helicopter gunships (which have the advantage of also being able to carry up to eight troopers) and light aircraft.

OTHER FORCES

The Russian political system is characterized by competition between powerful bureaucratic agencies and power blocs. This helps explain why, during and since the 1990s, there has been a proliferation of separate armed elements and other *spetsgruppy* attached to numerous ministries and agencies. In part this reflects the real challenges that they face, but it is also partly the result of a process of "bureaucratic warlordism," as rival bodies assert their strength and independence.

Military Police
Indiscipline, crime, embezzlement, and abuse of junior personnel within the Russian military have long been endemic problems that have eroded operational effectiveness, drained the defense budget, and encouraged draft-dodging on a very large scale. One reason for this has been the lack of a dedicated and properly trained military police force. Instead, regular military policing was simply the responsibility of the Commandant's Service

---

4 See Elite 194, *The Chinese People's Liberation Army since 1949: Ground Forces*

(which was largely a traffic-control body), or detachments from regular units on rotating duty. The Main Military Prosecutor's Office in Moscow was responsible for investigating serious crimes, but usually had to do so through local unit commands, providing ample scope for cover-ups. In 2011, Chief Military Prosecutor Sergei Fridinsky described the scope of military corruption as "mindboggling," and declared that perhaps 20 percent of all funds allocated to state defense disappeared through theft and kickbacks.

As a result, in 2010 it was announced that Russia was to establish its own Military Police (*Voennaya politsiya*, VP), to be led by LtGen Sergei Surovikin, a notoriously tough ex-*Spetsnaz* officer who had fought in Afghanistan, Tajikistan, and Chechnya. The first unit, a battalion of the Moscow-based 130th Independent Motor Rifle Brigade, was formally established in March 2012. The VP are scheduled to number 20,000, all volunteers, with brigade commands in each of the main military districts and fleet HQs: Baltiisk, Khabarovsk, Rostov-on-Don, St Petersburg, Sevastopol, Severomorsk, and Vladivostok.

Although there will be local variation depending on the size of the parent command, a typical VP brigade will number just over 2,500 effectives, organized into three mechanized infantry battalions. However, although broadly structured and equipped on regular military lines, they will not have heavy weapons. While they will have some BTR-80 armored personnel carriers, they will largely deploy in cars, trucks, and a combination of domestic GAZ-233034/233036 Tigr ("Tiger") and Italian Fiat Iveco M65 light armored vehicles. They will also include specialized elements, such as a psychological operations company and military divers.

President Putin and his close-protection team attending a wreath-laying ceremony at the Tomb of the Unknown Soldier on Victory Day. His bodyguards from the Presidential Security Service are among the most reliable and best-trained officers within the Russian security community. Typically, they would be armed with handguns and small submachine guns such as the PP-91 Kedr; this SMG is especially favored, since it can be worn in a large shoulder holster or carried under a coat. (Losevsky Photo & Video/Shutterstock.com)

1

2

2a

3

The Federal Protection Service

The Federal Protection Service (*Federalnaya sluzhba okhrany*, FSO) is simultaneously one of the most visible of Russia's security agencies – not least, as it provides the uniformed guards for the Kremlin, State Duma (parliament) and other government centers – yet also one of the least understood. It was formed in 1996 on the basis of the former Main Guard Directorate which, in turn, was a new incarnation of the KGB's Ninth Directorate, which had provided similar functions for the Soviet Party leadership. Its primary role is the physical protection of key officials and government buildings, and it comprises both the Presidential Security Service (*Sluzhba bezopasnosti prezidenta*, SBP) and the Presidential Regiment, also known as the Kremlin Guard.

The SBP provides bodyguards for the president, prime minister, and other dignitaries, and for government buildings. It includes close-protection officers, snipers, bomb-disposal experts, its own medical and counterintelligence teams, and also a platoon of divers who check any boats which VIPs will be boarding. Given that both Presidents Putin and Medvedev were also known for their enthusiasm for winter sports, the SBP also established a section of officers trained in skiing and mountain operations. The Presidential Squadron maintains four aircraft, and the Special Purpose Garage has a fleet of over a hundred cars, motorcycles, and vans, over and above those of *FGBU Transportnyi kombinat 'Rossiya,'* the state agency which provides the regular ground transport fleet for the Kremlin. The FSO Academy in Oryol trains recruits for all these elements.

A member of the Presidential Regiment wearing full dress uniform at the Tomb of the Unknown Soldier (see also Plate E2). The wave-green uniform is trimmed with bright blue facings and piping, and gold braid. Note the title "PREZIDENTSKII POLK" at the top of his sleeve, above the Federal Protection Service shoulder patch featuring the double-headed eagle, a sword, and a shield in the colors of the Russian flag. (Author's photo)

The FSO is also the Kremlin's answer to the age-old question "who guards the guardians?" Part of its role is to provide a final defense against any attempted coup by the military, MVD or FSB. More generally, its Special Communications & Information Service is not only responsible for the security and integrity of presidential communications, but also provides an alternative source of analysis of intelligence gathered by the other espionage agencies, notably the FSB, Foreign Intelligence Service (*Sluzhba vneshnoe razvedky*, SVR), and the Main Intelligence Directorate of the General Staff (*Glavnoe razvedyvatelnoe upravlenie*, GRU). The aim is to ensure that the Kremlin gets accurate and impartial briefings from them, and cannot be manipulated through the presentation of biased or deliberately partial intelligence.

The Presidential Regiment

This security force is housed within the Kremlin itself, taking up its historic Arsenal building (known to the FSO as Block 14). It is subordinated to the Kremlin Commandant, who himself reports directly to the director of the FSO. The *Prezidentsky Polk* is descended from the Latvian riflemen who guarded Lenin after the 1917 Revolution, and the cadets from the first Red Army military school who were also pressed into this role during the Russian Civil War.

Soldiers from the Presidential Regiment perform security duties throughout the Kremlin and also in Red Square, as well as providing the ceremonial guards for the Tomb of the Unknown Soldier in the adjacent Alexander Gardens. There they stage a carefully choreographed changing of the guard every hour, bearing elderly SKS rifles whose length is more suited to formal guard drill. For ceremonial duties the parade company wear resplendent uniforms introduced in 2006, based in color and style upon those of the old tsarist Imperial Guard, complete with shakos reminiscent of the Napoleonic period. Soldiers of the regiment usually wear more practical dark blue uniforms, however, and carry 5.45mm AKS-74U assault carbines, AKS-74 and AN-94 assault rifles, and high-powered 9mm SPS pistols. The regiment also has a disproportionate number of snipers, who increasingly use imported British AWM-F rifles chambered for the .338 Lapua Magnum round, as well as the domestically produced, customized Lobaev OVL-3 in .408 caliber.

This lieutenant of the Federal Protection Service, photographed near Lenin's Tomb on Red Square, wears the regular dark blue uniform with a bright blue welt down the trouser seam, here with a high-quality *ushanka* hat and a heavy winter jacket; note the gold rank stars on plain shoulder straps, and the FSO title and shoulder patch on the sleeve. The FSO is responsible for the security of key government buildings and officials; this officer carries a radio in his breast pocket and, under his jacket, a holstered SPS pistol. His role is essentially to provide eyes and ears on the public square; officers with more extensive and lethal weaponry are stationed just inside the Kremlin walls in case of trouble. (Author's photo)

The regiment comprises two infantry companies, a parade company, a cavalry escort squadron and a band. Overall it has a strength of 5,500 soldiers, a mix of draftees and professionals all of whom actively volunteer for the regiment. They need to meet demanding physical fitness requirements; to be at least 6ft 3in (190cm) tall; and to pass extensive background tests, which also exclude anyone with a criminal record, a close relative living abroad, or even simply having been registered at a psychiatric facility or a clinic for treating sexually transmitted disease or substance abuse.

The Justice Ministry

The Justice Ministry is responsible for the country's sprawling array of prisons, labor camps, and pre-trial detention centers, which is managed by the Federal Penitentiary Service (*Federalnaya sluzhba ispolneniya nakazanii*, FSIN – literally, "Federal Service for the Execution of Punishment"). Russia has one of the world's highest proportions of its population behind bars, and its prisons are notoriously overcrowded and under-maintained. In these circumstances it is hardly surprising that prison riots, sieges, and assaults are a relatively common occurrence. The majority are dealt with by regular FSIN wardens, sometimes assisted by the local police, but the service has also created its own *spetsgruppy* to tackle the most serious incidents and to apprehend the most dangerous escapees.

The first such unit was Fakel ("Torch"), established in Moscow. Given the size of the country, it soon became clear that it was not feasible for a single unit to deploy to prisons which might be half a day's flight away. Fakel became the Moscow region FSIN Special Designation Detachment (OSN), and others were created in regions and cities across the country. These include Zubr ("Bison") in Pskov, Krechet ("Falcon") in Izhevsk, Mangust ("Mongoose") in Samara, Akula ("Shark") in Krasnodar, Taifun ("Typhoon") in St Petersburg, Bely Medved ("White Bear") in the Republic of Sakha, Titan in Lipetsk, and Aisberg ("Iceberg") in Murmansk. Perhaps the best-known is Saturn, the Moscow City unit, which, like so many others, was also pressed into service during the Chechen campaigns; for example, in 1994 a force from Krechet was reportedly tasked with evacuating to Russia Chechen officials opposed to the rebel government.

Officers from Saturn, the Moscow City *spetsgruppa* of the Federal Penitentiary Service (FSIN), pose for a staged photo around a KAMAZ-43269 Vystrel ("Gunshot") armored car. They are armed respectively with a 9A-91 compact 9mm assault carbine fitted with a sound suppressor, an RPK-74M light machine gun, and a PYa pistol; note the use of the triangular side door for protection. The officers at left and right wear Saturn's standard green beret, but the major in the roof hatch has graduated from the strenuous training that entitles him to wear the prestigious red beret. (Vitaly Kuzmin)

These units undergo a tough training regime in armed and unarmed combat, negotiation, and psychological warfare, as well as deploying by foot, vehicle, rappelling, and helicopter insertion. Indeed, given the confused and often highly dangerous environments in which they must operate, even rivals such as the FSB and VV *Spetsnaz* grudgingly concede that the FSIN *spetsgruppy* are amongst the best at close-in operations. They are given considerable latitude over their personal weapons, and as well as standard-issue PMM, PYa, and GSh-18 pistols they increasingly use imported Glock 17s and 19s. Submachine guns are widely used, including the PP-91 and PP-2000, the AEK-919K, the PP-19, and the silenced 9A-91. For longer-range work they use assault rifles (especially the AN-91 and AK-74M) and sniper rifles (including the SVD, SV-98, OSV-96, and OVL-3). Their relative freedom to experiment has also seen them using such rare weapons as the Saiga 12-K automatic shotgun, and the bullpup OTs-03 SVU sniper rifle. They sometimes wear the blue "urban" camouflage often worn by regular FSIN wardens, or else green camouflage (especially when in pursuit of escapees in the countryside), but increasingly adopt modern black uniforms and body armor for assault missions.

F

FSIN, MCHS, & FSKN

(1) "Saturn" Group operator, Federal Penitentiary Service; Moscow, 2008

This member of the elite Saturn group of the FSIN prepares to resolve a hostage-taking in Moscow's infamous and overcrowded Butyrka prison. He is in full assault kit, with ZSh-1-2 helmet, Korund-VM vest, and leg and arm protectors. As well as his side-handled baton he has a holstered Glock 19 pistol, and a 9A-91 assault carbine. The 9A-91's sound suppressor makes it slightly unwieldy, but helps makes the launching and direction of an assault less obvious in the noisy environment of a prison riot.

(2) Robot technician, Ministry of Emergency Situations; Norilsk, 2010

This technician from the MChS prepares an MRK-27Kh robot for deployment into an area of potential toxic spill; designed for rescue and hazmat emergencies, this has a remote-control extending arm and carries video cameras, lights, and a variety of sensors to sample air pollution and radioactivity. The technician's greenish-blue MChS working uniform displays the MChS patch on both sleeves, below a Russian national patch on the left shoulder; a tab with the name of the ministry in Cyrillic script on her right breast, and her name tab and a repetition of the MChS bilingual cap patch on the left.

(3) "Grom" Group operator, Federal Narcotics Control Service; Kolomna, 2011

Grom ("Thunder") is the *spetsgruppa* of the Moscow directorate of the FSKN. This operator is wearing the SPOSN Spekter-S camouflage battledress newly released in 2010, with the Grom patch set at a slant on his right sleeve; the left sleeve would show the FSKN's badge of a snake transfixed on a sword. He has Kora-Kulon body armor; his weapons are a PP-19 Bizon SMG, and a PYa pistol in a thigh-holster rig.

The former oil billionaire Viktor Khodokovsky, once one of the richest men in Russia, stands in a bulletproof glass box during his trial in 2005 on charges of fraud and tax evasion. He is flanked by two members of the FSIN wearing four-color streaked camouflage fatigues over matching T-shirts. Note the star on cap cockades of two different types; the triple metal chevrons on the right-hand NCO's shoulder-strap slide; the wreathed star collar badges; the national patch on the left sleeve, and the FSIN patch on the right. (kojoku/Shutterstock.com)

OTHER MINISTRIES & AGENCIES

The **Federal Narcotics Control Service** (*Federalnaya sluzhba po kontrolyu za oborotom narkotikov*, FSKN), founded in 2003, is a national law-enforcement agency broadly comparable to the US Drug Enforcement Administration. Among its total of 34,000 plainclothes and uniformed personnel are a number of small *spetsgruppy*, many of which go by the generic name of SOBR. These are responsible for spearheading especially hazardous operations, usually alongside police special forces. The premier special unit is Grom ("Thunder"), based in Moscow. Given just how well-armed, violent, and powerful some Russian organized-crime gangs can be, FSKN *Spetsnaz* go through similar training to many other such units; it is significant that their first chief was a veteran of the FSB's Alpha. Additionally, they reportedly also receive unusually extensive legal training, so as to ensure that the outcomes of their operations will be upheld in court.

Officially, the **Foreign Intelligence Service** (SVR) has had no *spetsgruppy* since it lost Vympel in 1993. However, in 1998 a new unit, Zaslon ("Shield" or "Back-up") was secretly established to provide armed support for SVR operations abroad. The Russian government has never admitted the unit's existence, but from those reports that have surfaced it seems to have perhaps 300 members, and can carry out a wide range of covert missions, from embassy security in extreme circumstances through to assassination. Western intelligence sources have connected Zaslon with a spate of murders in Europe and elsewhere of Chechens raising funds for the rebel cause, for example, as well as reprisal attacks on terrorists targeting Russian diplomats and nationals overseas.

The rise of heavily armed and violent poachers has even forced agencies involved in forestry and fishery protection to found their own paramilitary squads. In 2009, for example, Rosrybolovstvo, the **Russian Fishery Agency**, announced not only that it was arming its fisheries inspectors, increasing their number from 3,000 to 4,500, and even buying drones to provide airborne surveillance, but would establish a quick-reaction force. Recruited from a mix of fisheries inspectors and veteran soldiers, this could be deployed to fight poachers in particularly difficult places such as Dagestan, where the poaching of sturgeon, the source of highly priced caviar, has become a criminal industry.

Such *spetsgruppy* are not always so martial, however. The **Ministry of Emergency Situations** (*Ministerstvo po chrezvychainym situatsiyam*, MChS – sometimes known in the West as EMERCOM, for Emergency Control Ministry) is responsible for a wide range of agencies, including the national ambulance and firefighting services and civil defense and disaster relief. To this end it also includes *Tsentrospas*, an elite central rapid-response airmobile search-and-rescue force. With its own facilities near Moscow's Ramenskoye airbase, its teams can deploy within 30–60 minutes if using helicopters, or up to three hours when they must use fixed-wing aircraft. The 650 personnel include highly trained specialists ranging from mountain-rescue teams and paramedics to divers and dog-handlers, many of them trained for deployment by helicopter or parachute, and to operate autonomously in the field for up to two weeks. *Tsentrospas* also drives much research into new search-and-rescue equipment in Russia; it was, for example, a key customer behind the development of the Kamov Ka-226 "Sergei," a light utility helicopter with interchangeable mission pods that enable its use as an ambulance, cargo-hauler, firefighting aircraft or simply personnel transport.

Perhaps the most problematic experiment in "paramilitarization" was the short-lived **Tax Police** (*Nalogovaya politsiya*, NP). Formed in 1993 as an arm of the Federal Tax Service, their role was to address the chronic underpayment

The Ministry of Emergency Situations (MChS) controls all Russia's emergency fire, rescue, and medical services, and also maintains semi-militarized emergency-response elements; this officer's shoulder boards bear ranking equivalent to an Army captain. The MChS greenish-blue uniform (see also Plate F2) is sometimes worn with an orange beret on dress occasions but more usually, as here, with a field cap. The cap patch bears both Cyrillic and English-language "EMERCOM" titles around the tricolor-and-star insignia; here the English title is repeated on the right breast tab, and his right sleeve displays the patch of the State Firefighting Service. (Losevsky Photo & Video/ Shutterstock.com)

An example of the Mil Mi-26T, the largest helicopter in the world, in MChS livery. The ministry employs them in a variety of roles, from flying cranes, to airlift for *Tsentrospas* emergency-response teams and supplies to disaster areas, and, in the Mi-26TP variant, for firefighting. (Vitaly Kuzmin)

of taxes that was starving the Russian treasury: at the time it was estimated that a quarter of all taxes went unpaid. In a bid to kill two birds with one stone, many of the new NP officers had been members of the former KGB's Fifth Chief Directorate, responsible for monitoring and suppressing internal dissent. Worried that these unemployed secret policemen might form dangerous alliances with organized crime or remnants of the old Soviet order, Boris Yeltsin opted to give them jobs in the NP. However, the idea was clearly not thought through: the NP was deliberately underfunded, and instead was to rely on a bounty that it would receive from all additional tax revenues it could collect. On one level the NP was successful, since it certainly brought in extra resources to the treasury; as a result it grew steadily, from an original strength of 12,000 officers to 21,500 by 1994, and 53,000 by the late 1990s. On the other hand, the combination of personnel whose background was in political repression, wide powers almost beyond control by the courts, and a reliance on bounties, had wholly predictable consequences.

The black-uniformed officers of this predatory force, typically wearing full paramilitary kit, became a familiar and hated scourge of companies in the main cities, and increasingly operated more like protection racketeers than revenue agents. Given that the tax system in the 1990s was still being converted from the Soviet code to one fit for a market economy, it was extraordinarily complex and often contradictory. As a result, the NP would often raid a company and threaten to conduct a full audit, which would consume considerable time and resources for the company in question, after which it was likely that the NP would uncover some underpayment. Alternatively, the company could suddenly "realize" that it had failed to pay an agreed amount of tax, and after money changed hands the NP would be on their way. The consequence was a growing chorus of complaint and evidence that the NP was increasingly plagued by corruption – not least because businesspeople would bribe them to harass commercial rivals. As a result, in 2003 the Tax Police was abolished as a separate service, with most of its officers being reassigned to the MVD or FSKN.

G NORTH CAUCASUS

(1) Captain, 46th Brigade, Interior Troops; Second Chechen War, 2006

This captain from the VV 46th Bde is deployed in the mountains of southern Chechnya, commanding a patrol seeking to interdict the flow of weapons and sympathizers across the border from Georgia. Instead of the usual VV camouflage fatigues he is wearing a Gorka Bars mountain suit, and a simple bandana on his head. Kneepads are increasingly common issue for VV personnel, but he may well have bought these privately. He has an AK-74M rifle with under-barrel GP-25 grenade-launcher and 1PN51 second-generation night sight, and (obscured in this pose) a non-standard holster rig for a PYa pistol as a back-up weapon. As is appropriate for such operations, he does not wear any colorful patches or even rank insignia.

(2) Private, Interior Troops; Chechnya, 2002

Victory in counterinsurgency warfare often depends upon quickly laying down devastating firepower before insurgents can melt into cover. The AGS-17 Plamya ("Flame") automatic grenade-launcher performs that purpose admirably; it may be heavy and clumsy, but it can rapid-fire 30mm VOG-17M high-explosive fragmentation grenades in a direct or indirect trajectory. This VV soldier wears ANA Noch 91M forest *kamysh* battledress without insignia. His *ushanka* is not just warm – its flaps also offer ear-protection against the AGS-17's roar. In combat he would just pull on his old-fashioned SSh-68 steel helmet over it.

(3) General Rashid Nurgaliyev, Interior Minister; Grozny, 2008

Russia's Interior Minister from 2003 to 2012, Rashid Nurgaliyev regularly visited the North Caucasus; this image is from photos taken during a visit in April 2008. Whereas he would often wear battle fatigues, on that occasion – in an effort to suggest that the situation in Chechnya had been normalized – he wore his regular service uniform as a four-star general of the MVD. The large crown of the service cap bears the MVD's double-headed eagle crest above the general officers' version of the MVD star badge; the right sleeve patch is that of the MVD Central Apparatus, and the "Russia/tricolor/MVD" patch is worn on the left sleeve, though hidden at this angle. Nurgaliyev was a political survivor, but unpopular within the MVD; in 2012 he was replaced with Gen Vladimir Kolokoltsev, former head of the Moscow police.

GUNS FOR THE MASSES

The forces of order

A *starshina* (a rank equivalent to sergeant-major) of the Moscow police's Extradepartmental Guard Service, its "contract" security arm which hires out the services of police officers; in this case he is guarding the main buildings of the General Prosecutor's Office on Bolshaya Dmitrovka Street. He wears the blue-gray regular police uniform with a red trouser welt, his rank indicated by the broad central stripe along his shoulder straps. Over the jacket he wears a light tactical vest displaying the winged owl symbol of the Extradepartmental Guard; he is armed with a PMM pistol, a baton, and (obscured here) a slung PP-2000 submachine gun. (Author's photo)

The proliferation of armed muscle across many government agencies has also been reflected in society as a whole. Facing a continued problem of violent and well-armed organized crime, many companies have turned to a sometimes equally violent and well-armed private security sector, leading to the rise of virtual private armies. At their peak in the late 1990s the largest four companies in Moscow alone employed a total of more than 8,000 armed operators. Since then the industry has become less freewheeling and more regulated (including greater constraints on private security officers' use of weapons), but as of 2011 it was still a massive business sector, worth US $7 billion annually. Pervasive reports have suggested that these guards are often used by private individuals and companies as hired muscle – for instance, for dispersing environmental protesters, breaking strikes, and hounding investigative journalists. However, it must be admitted that they also provide very real and necessary services, as well as legal employment opportunities for military and police veterans who might otherwise be tempted down murkier paths. This is also a sector to which the police themselves have staked a claim; the MVD's Okhrana ("Guard") corporation earns the ministry an official profit of almost US $7 million each year.

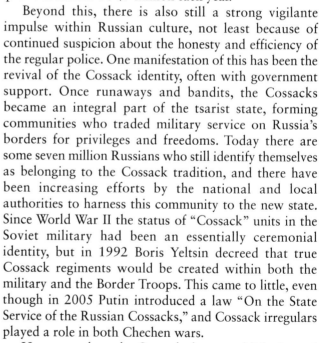

Beyond this, there is also still a strong vigilante impulse within Russian culture, not least because of continued suspicion about the honesty and efficiency of the regular police. One manifestation of this has been the revival of the Cossack identity, often with government support. Once runaways and bandits, the Cossacks became an integral part of the tsarist state, forming communities who traded military service on Russia's borders for privileges and freedoms. Today there are some seven million Russians who still identify themselves as belonging to the Cossack tradition, and there have been increasing efforts by the national and local authorities to harness this community to the new state. Since World War II the status of "Cossack" units in the Soviet military had been an essentially ceremonial identity, but in 1992 Boris Yeltsin decreed that true Cossack regiments would be created within both the military and the Border Troops. This came to little, even though in 2005 Putin introduced a law "On the State Service of the Russian Cossacks," and Cossack irregulars played a role in both Chechen wars.

However, where the Cossacks have established a real role is in security and policing work. By 1997 Cossack companies were working for the Moscow city government, for example, and Cossack patrols and units have also been raised in several areas of the Caucasus and the Russian Far East. The model varies quite widely; for instance, at the most basic level, a December 2012 report in *The Times* of London noted that Cossacks led by one

Igor Gulichev had been assigned a "neighborhood watch" role at Moscow's Belarusskaya rail station to discourage unlicensed peddlers, in return for free bus passes instead of wages. In the main, Cossack volunteers are provided with stipends, uniforms, equipment, and sometimes either guns or gun permits, in return for providing security in particular regions. Often wearing uniforms reminiscent of their tsarist forebears (and sometimes even carrying the infamous *nagayka*, a short horse-whip that can be used just as easily on people), they are an increasingly visible – if unpredictable and under-regulated – element of the Russian security scene.

Forces of disorder

There are also powerful and often well-armed elements on the other side of the fence. Russian organized crime remains sophisticated, powerful, and ubiquitous, but it is no longer the obvious force that it was in the 1990s. In that anarchic decade gangsters could openly flaunt their underworld status, and violence on the streets was a constant. The arrival of Putin to the presidency in 2000 did not lead to an all-out crackdown on organized crime, but it did quickly become clear that the state was not willing to accept the overt disorder that had previously reigned. Since then, organized criminal violence has not disappeared but it has become more discriminating. Contract killings, for example, remain a staple of criminal-business culture, but instead of being delivered through car bombs and drive-by shootings in public places, they tend to be precisely targeted, with only the victim and maybe his (or occasionally her) driver or bodyguard falling to the assassin's bullets. A recent example was the assassination of one of the last of the true godfathers, "Grandfather Khasan." The 75-year-old Aslan Rashidovich Usoyan, an ethnic

Private security guards from the commercial Rus' agency watch military vehicles pass during rehearsals for a parade. Their dark police-style uniform and red-and-gold sleeve and back patches reflect the extent to which these security firms are offshoots from various government agencies. For example, veterans from the Alpha antiterrorist unit formed their own "Alpha-A" (ChOP) private security company. (Author's photo)

Cossack cadets from the Kuban Host parade in Krasnodar in 2012. Some 7,000 Cossacks from Krasnodar Region, Adygeya, and Karachayevo-Cherkessia took part in this, one of the largest shows of Cossack pride in post-Soviet times. Their uniforms are dark blue with red trouser-stripes; the red shoulder boards bear the gold letters "KK" for "Cossack cadet." (Anna Martynova/Shutterstock.com)

Kurd from Georgia, was shot dead on January 16, 2013 while leaving Moscow's Karetny Dvor restaurant by a rooftop sniper with an AS Val silenced rifle. This killing may have been associated with feuding over the anticipated underworld profits from the 2014 Winter Olympics in Sochi.

In the 1990s, before this relative "professionalization" of the assassin's trade, what were known in *mafiya* slang as the *byk* ("bull") and the *torpedo* were two commonly encountered characters, the first being the well-muscled thug, the second the killer. In the new era of less-visible organized crime, many of these types have been converted into "private security guards," or simply have less of a role. Nonetheless, there remains a small cadre of professional assassins, who are typically freelancers not associated with any of the main gangs or networks. One example was Alexander Solonik, nicknamed "Alexander the Great" or "Alexander the Macedonian," after his supposed penchant for using a pistol in each hand – known in Russia as "Macedonian-style" shooting. A former member of the Army's *Spetsnaz* and then the OMON, he was dismissed from the police for indiscipline, and in 1987 was convicted of rape. He escaped from a labor camp and soon drifted into the underworld, becoming a killer for hire. He specialized in assassinating well-guarded criminal "godfathers": he would later confess to killing three, although there is reason to believe that his tally was rather higher. When Solonik was arrested in 1994 he fought his way out of a police station, killing five officers and two security guards before finally being recaptured. Again managing to break out of prison, he fled the country and settled in Greece, where he was eventually murdered in a revenge attack in 1997 by a team of killers from the Orekhovskaya-Medvedkovskaya gang.

Beyond these relatively workaday criminal gangsters, more formidable armed forces have also arisen to fight Moscow. Chechnya is the obvious case in point, but as the war there subsides the focus of the nationalist-jihadist insurgency against Russian rule has shifted to the other republics of the North Caucasus. However, these *jamaats* (as the insurgent groups are known) are essentially outside the scope of this book.

H: NORTH CAUCASUS

(1) Chechen soldier, Vostok Battalion; Georgia, 2008

The last major operation before disbandment of the Vostok ("East") Battalion, a Chechen unit assembled from followers of the Yamadayev clan under the wing of Russian Military Intelligence (GRU), was its deployment in South Ossetia during the 2008 Russian invasion of Georgia. This soldier typifies the mix of professional toughness and irregular style for which they were known. He is wearing M21 pattern jacket and trousers in woodland Flora camouflage; as an ex-paratrooper of the Russian Army he proudly wears their *telnyashka* T-shirt, and some men fixed to a breast pocket their old Army blood-group patches. The red tassel draws attention to the personal fighting knife tucked into the side of his Tarzan M21 assault vest, but his main weapon is an AKS-74 assault rifle with GP-25 grenade-launcher.

(2) Senior sergeant, Kadyrov Special Purpose Police Regiment; Grozny, 2011

This NCO from the Chechen MVD special police regiment created by the Kadyrov clan is manning one of the many checkpoints in and around Grozny. The uniform is unique to the Chechens, a mix of police and military styles with right-sleeve insignia showing the regimental patch below the Chechen-language title "Grozny," its location. His breast tab reads "Russia MVD." He is wearing the Chechen MVD full dress cockade badge on his olive beret – a widespread unofficial practice within the regiment, which flaunted its elite status. He carries an AKS-74 rifle, obscuring here a PMM pistol holstered at his belt.

(3) South Ossetian irregular; Gori, 2008

When Russian forces invaded Georgia in 2008 they were supported by South Ossetian irregulars. This fighter, fresh from raids on the suburbs of the town of Gori, wears an old one-piece KLMK Berezka camouflage suit as once worn by Soviet scouts and snipers, with a mismatched M23 Pioner utility vest. A lower sleeve patch in the South Ossetian colors is an unusual touch. He has also used some Flora-patterned material to fashion a crude masked balaclava; hiding their faces was common practice amongst irregulars engaged in cross-border and reprisal attacks on civilians. He is carrying an eclectic range of weapons: a PK GPMG, an elderly AKM-47 assault rifle, and, tucked into his vest, an even more dated Tokarev pistol.

This GAZ-233034 SPM-1 Tigr ("Tiger") armored car bears the livery of the Moscow OMON riot police (since this photo was taken the "MILITSIYA" on the blue stripe has been replaced with "POLITSIYA"). This powerful vehicle, with exceptional cross-country capability, is also in regular military service; its value in an urban setting is less apparent. (Vitaly Kuzmin).

TOOLS OF THE TRADE

In the early years of post-Soviet Russia the security forces were unable to import equipment for both political and financial reasons, and were instead forced to rely upon often dated or improvised domestic items. More recently, however, many Russian companies have risen to the challenge of producing world-class weapons and kit, and resources have also been made available for at least the *spetsgruppy* to import what they need for their work. The previous descriptions of various units note the use of such imports, but what follows is a brief overview of some of the domestically produced weapons in use. The days when Russian forces fielded a relatively narrow range of standard-issue products of a few monolithic state arms factories are long since over. The Russian defense industry is increasingly diversified, with new lines and manufacturers emerging to meet numerous real and potential needs, and the proliferation of large and small *spetsgruppy* under different agencies and with varying roles has also encouraged a more mission-specific approach to weapons procurement.

Pistols

The venerable Russian 9x18mm Makarov PM remains in use, especially amongst police and lower-status forces. It is a compact design, but relatively underpowered and short-ranged, and even the modernized PMM model – with higher-powered ammunition and a 12-round rather than 8-round magazine – is currently being phased out. The new standard police and military sidearm is the 9x19mm 6P35 Yarygin PYa Grach, a much more modern weapon, although this is supplemented by a wide range of domestic and imported pistols. One of the former is the four-barreled PB-4SP OSA "traumatic pistol" firing non-lethal rubber rounds. At the other end of the spectrum is the 9x21mm Serdyukov SPS, a weapon designed to defeat body armor.

Russia retains a particular expertise in special-role weapons, of which the SPP-1M underwater handgun and PSS silenced pistol are good examples. The SPP-1M is a particularly distinctive weapon: a four-barreled pistol firing long, drag-stabilized 4.5x40mm rounds with a lethal range of 5–20m (16–66ft) depending on depth under water. The PSS looks like a stubby, conventional semi-automatic pistol, but was designed by the Soviets to be as close as possible to a truly silent weapon for covert kills. It uses a unique subsonic 7.62x42mm round containing an internal piston in the casing that seals the cartridge when the bullet is discharged, keeping in the sound and blast. The six-shot pistol has an effective range of little more than 25m (82ft) and little armor-piercing capacity, but when fired it has no more report than an air pistol.

Submachine guns

Perhaps the greatest variety is evident in the range of submachine guns used. The AKS-74U, a shortened assault carbine version of the regular AK-74 rifle, is widely employed, especially by police units, but is not generally considered an appropriate weapon for special forces. It is convenient to handle, and can lay down a serious volume of fire, but it is not especially accurate, and thus wastes the superior training of *spetsgruppy*. Its 5.45mm round can also be a danger to innocent bystanders during law-enforcement operations, as it has been known to penetrate walls or pass through the target. Consequently, the 1990s saw Russia's police and military looking for SMGs using less powerful 9mm pistol rounds and configured for covert and special operations. This spawned a bewildering array of weapons. These range from small and easily concealed weapons such as the PP-91 Kedr ("Cedar"), PP-9 Klin ("Wedge"), and OTs-02 Kiparis ("Cypress"), which are really machine pistols, through larger personal-defense types like the PP-2000 and the less widely used AEK-919K Kashtan ("Chestnut"), to SMGs like the 9A-91, which is really an assault carbine albeit firing 9mm rounds.

Many of these weapons show a Russian desire to experiment with new ideas, such as the PP-19 Bizon ("Bison"), a light weapon with a distinctive tubular magazine along the barrel holding 64 rounds, which reduces the risk of the weapon snagging if produced from under a coat. These were not always successful, however, and the PP-19 in particular received a mixed reception in the field. The Vityaz *spetsgruppa* even requested a new, more conventional weapon, and the Izhevsk works produced the PP-19-01 Vityaz model, essentially an AKS-74U rechambered in 9mm. Likewise the PP-90, a weapon that folded down into a box that could be carried in a large coat pocket for covert operations, proved so unreliable that it was withdrawn from service.

Operators in the more elite security units have both the budgets to buy personal kit of their choice, and also greater freedom to customize issued equipment. This OMSN police commando carries an Austrian Glock pistol provided by his unit, in a personally acquired Blackhawk SERPA Close Quarter Combat holster rig. (Vitaly Kuzmin)

Rifles

The standard assault rifle is still the AKM-74, a 5.45mm advanced version of the ubiquitous AK-47 Kalashnikov. The AK-74 was first introduced in 1979, and was succeeded from 1991 by the AKM-74 (M = *modernizirovanniy*, "modernized"). It is available with a range of accessories, from underslung grenade-launchers to various day and night sights. While dated, it is still a workmanlike weapon and remains in general use amongst the regular armed forces, as budget constraints have thwarted attempts to replace it with something more modern.

Increasingly *spetsgruppy* are using a variety of other weapons, although so far these are generally Russian-made. The AK-103 is essentially an AK-74 firing the older 7.62mm round, favored by some units for its greater stopping power. The AK-107 is externally similar to the AK-74 and fires the same round, but has a recoil reduction system that makes it much more controllable. This virtue is shared by the AN-94, which was meant to replace the AKM-74 in general service but so far has only been issued to various elite units. Even rarer is the OTs-14-4A Groza ("Thunderstorm"), a compact 9mm bullpup weapon based on the AKS-74U platform. In keeping with the Russians' penchant for silenced weapons, they also deploy the AS Val ("Shaft"); understandably designated *Avtomat Spetsialyi*, "Specialized Assault Rifle," this heavy-barreled carbine fires subsonic 9mm SP-6 armor-piercing rounds to an effective range of 200–300m (660–990 feet).

Likewise, the *spetsgruppy* will in appropriate circumstances use the VSS Vintorez silenced sniper's rifle, which has an effective range of up to 400m (1,320 feet), but longer-ranged and more hard-hitting weapons are generally preferred. Lower-status units have to make do with the veteran Dragunov SVD, a weapon derived from the Kalashnikov and not up to modern standards of precision. As a result, more elite units quickly turned to

Some of the weapons used by *spetsgruppy*. From left to right: a VSK-94 silenced sniper rifle; a bullpup OTs-03 SVU sniper rifle; and a 9mm PP-2000 submachine gun, with Zenit-4TK laser sight and tactical light. (Vitaly Kuzmin)

alternatives. Most of these are domestically produced, but the British Accuracy International AWM-F has also won a very loyal constituency amongst marksmen in Alpha and the Presidential Guard Service. Russian-built rifles include the bolt-action SV-98, and the bullpup OTs-03 SVU (*Snaiperskaya Vintovka Ukorochennaya*, "shortened sniper rifle") based on a highly modified SVD frame. Perhaps the most prestigious of all the available rifles are custom-made Lobaev OVL-3s, and their accuracy has become the benchmark by which Russian marksmen measure other weapons. Finally, in keeping with other nations, the Russians have come to appreciate the value of a large-caliber anti-material rifle for devastating long-range firepower. The OSV-96 is a 12.7mm weapon that first saw action in a countersniper context in Chechnya; it has an effective range of 1,200m (1,320 yards) against a human, and 1,800m (2,000 yards) against larger targets.

Other weapons
When appropriate, these forces also have full access to a range of heavier weapons. The Interior Troops, especially the ODON and ObrON, are fully militarized, and are therefore armed with a range of support weapons, especially machine guns and AGS-17 grenade-launchers. At the other end of the spectrum, beyond a variety of rigid and flexible batons and the PB-4SP pistol, security units have access to an array of gas and stun munitions, including the Drofa "flash-bang" stun grenade, the Dreyf-2 tear-gas grenade, and the Cheremukha-10M incapacitating aerosol spray. Taser weapons are also beginning to be introduced for police use. Shotguns are not widely used outside the FSIN, being primarily Saiga semi-automatic weapons (based on the Kalashnikov) and older KZ-23s. Beyond these, public-order forces have access to a range of modern water cannon, including the formidable Lavina-Uragan.

Photographed in 2011, this operator from Rys', the Moscow police OMSN unit (redesignated that year as a KSN), is taking part in a fiercely contested competition between police and security special-operations groups, the Spetsnaz Triathlon. Over his "SS-style" camouflage fatigues and black body-armor vest he wears a rappelling harness. Note also the tactical gloves with reinforced knuckles, which pack an extra punch in hand-to-hand combat. (Vitaly Kuzmin)

Body armor

Body armor was used by the Red Army in modest quantities during World War II, but thereafter was long neglected by the Soviets. Examples began to see widespread use during their ill-fated war in Afghanistan (1979–89), but these remained relatively heavy, clumsy, and ineffective. Strides have been made since then, with a range of both lighter and heavier vests and other protective kit available for different types of duty. The distinctive metal-visored helmet worn by some operators, typically a Maska or Sfera design, is increasingly out of favor for its lack of comfort and the limits it places on hearing and vision, and instead modern composite designs with goggles or clear shields are now preferred.

SELECT BIBLIOGRAPHY

Boltunov, M., *Al'fa: Sverkhsekretnaya otryad KGB* (Moscow, 1992)

Boltunov, M., *Vympel: ne oruzhiem edinym* (Moscow, 2006)

Desmond, D., *Camouflage Uniforms of the Soviet Union and Russia: 1937 to the Present* (Atglen, PA, 1998)

Makarov, S., *Spetsnaz FSB Rossii. Porokh i tuman* (Minsk, 2011)

Soldatov, A. & Borogan, I., *The New Nobility* (New York, 2010)

INDEX

References to illustrations and plates are shown in **bold**. Captions to plates are shown in brackets.